W9-ANU-132

Major Muslim Nations

Malaysia

Major Muslim Nations

Major Muslim Nations

Malaysia

Barbara Aoki Poisson

Mason Crest Publishers
Philadelphia

Mason Crest Publishers
370 Reed Road
Broomall, PA 19008
www.masoncrest.com

First printing

1 3 5 7 9 8 6 4 2

Library of Congress Cataloging-in-Publication Data

Poisson, Barbara Aoki.
    Malaysia / Barbara Aoki Poisson.
        p. cm. — (Major Muslim Nations)
    Previously published: 2005.
    Includes bibliographical references and index.
    ISBN 978-1-4222-1409-1 (hardcover : alk. paper)
    ISBN 978-1-4222-1439-8 (pbk. : alk. paper)
    1. Malaysia—Juvenile literature. I. Title.
    DS592.P64 2008
    959.5—dc22

                                        2008033767

Original ISBN: 1-59084-838-1 (hc)

Major Muslim Nations

Table of Contents

Malaysian women walk to Masjid Negeri, the state mosque of Melaka.

Dr. Harvey Sicherman, president and director of the Foreign Policy Research Institute, is the author of such books as *America the Vulnerable: Our Military Problems and How to Fix Them* (2002) and *Palestinian Autonomy, Self-Government and Peace* (1993).

Introduction

by Dr. Harvey Sicherman

America's triumph in the Cold War promised a new burst of peace and prosperity. Indeed, the decade between the demise of the Soviet Union and the destruction of September 11, 2001, seems in retrospect deceptively attractive. Today, of course, we are more fully aware—to our sorrow—of the dangers and troubles no longer just below the surface.

The Muslim identities of most of the terrorists at war with the United States have also provoked great interest in Islam and the role of religion in politics. A truly global religion, Islam's tenets are held by hundreds of millions of people from every ethnic group, scattered across the globe. It is crucial for Americans not to assume that Osama bin Laden's ideas are identical to those of most Muslims, or, for that matter, that most Muslims are Arabs. Also, it is important for Americans to understand the "hot spots" in the Muslim world because many will make an impact on the United States.

A glance at the map establishes the extraordinary coverage of our authors. Every climate and terrain may be found and every form of human

society, from the nomads of the Central Asian steppes and Arabian deserts to highly sophisticated cities such as Cairo and Singapore. Economies range from barter systems to stock exchanges, from oil-rich countries to the thriving semi-market powers, such as India, now on the march. Others have built wealth on service and shipping.

The Middle East and Central Asia are heavily armed and turbulent. Pakistan is a nuclear power, Iran threatens to become one, and Israel is assumed to possess a small arsenal. But in other places, such as Afghanistan and the Sudan, the horse and mule remain potent instruments of war. All have a rich history of conflict, domestic and international, old and new.

Governments include dictatorships, democracies, and hybrids without a name; centralized and decentralized administrations; and older patterns of tribal and clan associations. The region is a veritable encyclopedia of political expression.

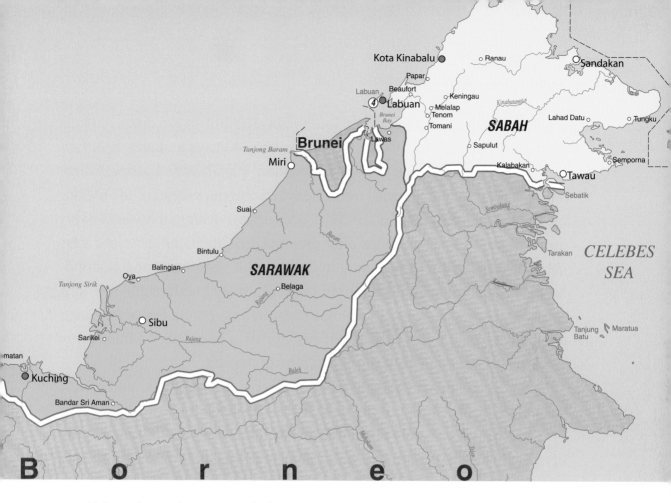

Although such variety defies easy generalities, it is still possible to make several observations.

First, the regional geopolitics reflect the impact of empires and the struggles of post-imperial independence. While centuries-old history is often invoked, the truth is that the modern Middle East political system dates only from the 1920s, when the Ottoman Empire dissolved in the wake of its defeat by Britain and France in World War I. States such as Algeria, Iraq, Israel, Jordan, Kuwait, Saudi Arabia, Syria, Turkey, and the United Arab Emirates did not exist before 1914—they became independent between 1920 and 1971. Others, such as Egypt and Iran, were dominated by foreign powers until well after World War II. Few of the leaders of these states were happy with the territories they were assigned or the borders, which were often drawn by Europeans. Yet the system has endured despite many efforts to change it.

A similar story may be told in South Asia. The British Raj dissolved into India and Pakistan in 1947. Still further east, Malaysia shares a British experience but Indonesia, a Dutch invention, has its own European heritage. These imperial histories weigh heavily upon the politics of the region.

The second observation concerns economics, demography, and natural resources. These countries offer dramatic geographical contrasts: vast parched deserts and high mountains, some with year-round snow; stone-hard volcanic rifts and lush semi-tropical valleys; extremely dry and extremely wet conditions, sometimes separated by only a few miles; large permanent rivers and wadis, riverbeds dry as a bone until winter rains send torrents of flood from the mountains to the sea.

Although famous historically for its exports of grains, fabrics, and spices, most recently the Muslim regions are known more for a single commodity: oil. Petroleum is unevenly distributed; while it is largely concentrated in the Persian Gulf and Arabian Peninsula, large oil fields can be found in Algeria, Libya, and further east in Indonesia. Natural gas is also abundant in the Gulf, and there are new, potentially lucrative offshore gas fields in the Eastern Mediterranean.

This uneven distribution of wealth has been compounded by demographics. Birth rates are very high, but the countries with the most oil are often lightly populated. Over the last decade, a youth "bulge" has emerged and this, combined with increased urbanization, has strained water supplies, air quality, public sanitation, and health services throughout the Muslim world. How will these young people be educated? Where will they work? A large outward migration, especially to Europe, indicates the lack of opportunity at home.

In the face of these challenges, the traditional state-dominated economic strategies have given way partly to experiments with "privatization" and foreign investment. But economic progress has come slowly, if at all, and most people have yet to benefit from "globalization," although there are pockets of prosperity, high technology (notably in Israel), and valuable natural resources (oil, gas, and minerals). Rising expectations have yet to be met.

A third important observation is the role of religion in the Middle East. Americans, who take separation of church and state for granted, should know that most countries in the region either proclaim their countries to be Muslim or allow a very large role for that religion in public life. (Islamic law, Sharia, permits people to practice Judaism and Christianity in Muslim states but only as *dhimmi*, "protected" but second-class citizens.) Among those with predominantly Muslim populations, Turkey alone describes itself as secular and prohibits avowedly religious parties in the political system. Lebanon was a Christian-dominated state, and Israel continues to be a Jewish state. Even where politics are secular, religion plays an enormous role in culture, daily life, and legislation.

Islam has deeply affected every state and people in these regions. But Islamic practices and groups vary from the well-known Sunni and Shiite groups to energetic Salafi (Wahhabi) and Sufi movements. Over the last 20 years especially, South and Central Asia have become battlegrounds for competing Shiite (Iranian) and Wahhabi (Saudi) doctrines, well financed from abroad and aggressively antagonistic toward non-Muslims and each other. Resistance to the Soviet war in Afghanistan brought these groups battle-tested warriors and organizers responsive to the doctrines made popular by Osama bin Laden and others. This newly significant struggle within Islam, superimposed on an older Muslim history, will shape political and economic destinies throughout the region and beyond.

We hope that these books will enlighten both teacher and student about the critical "hot spots" of the Muslim world. These countries would be important in their own right to Americans; arguably, after 9/11, they became vital to our national security. And the enduring impact of Islam is a crucial factor we must understand. We at the Foreign Policy Research Institute hope these books will illuminate both the facts and the prospects.

Palm trees rise above the domes and minaret of a mosque in Kuala Lumpur, the largest city in Malaysia. Most of the 24 million residents of this country in Southeast Asia are Muslims.

1

Place in the World

$\mathcal{M}$alaysia is one of the most racially and religiously diverse nations in the Islamic world. This warm tropical land, blessed with a treasure trove of natural resources, is a dynamic blend of tradition and technology. The country was founded at the crossroads of one of the world's most vital sea routes between the Indian and Pacific oceans. For centuries, trade in the East was centered around the Malacca Strait. Today this vital sea lane, which is bordered by Malaysia, Singapore, and the Indonesian island of Sumatra, remains strategically significant. Each day one-third of the world's sea traffic passes through the narrow strait, carrying oil, timber, and other vital goods to global markets.

Trade played a large part in shaping the history of Malaysia. As early as the first century A.D., seaborne traders from China and India stopped at communities throughout the Malay Archipelago. Along with gold and other goods, these early traders brought highly influential traditions, religions, arts, and political philosophies. The centuries of trade also affected Malaysia's ethnic composition, and today the nation's population is primarily composed of ethnic Malays, Chinese, and Indians.

Islam became the dominant religion of Malaysia because of the importance of Melaka, a trading port located in a strategic spot along the Malacca Strait. An exiled Sumatran prince named Parameswara founded Melaka in 1400, and within a few decades it emerged as the richest and most powerful trading port in the East. In 1414, Parameswara married a Muslim princess from Indonesia; he accepted her religion, which had supplanted Hinduism and Buddhism as the dominant faith of the Indonesian archipelago. Most of the people of Melaka adopted the religion of their ruler, and this would have a significant impact on Malaysia's future. As Islam spread throughout the region, traders from other parts of the Muslim world flocked to Melaka, bringing the city international prestige.

As Melaka prospered, it attracted the attention of powerful European nations such as Portugal, the Netherlands, and England. During the early 16th century, the Portuguese captured Melaka and other ports in the Indian Ocean, launching an era of European domination that would last until the mid-20th century. Melaka changed hands many times as European nations struggled to dominate the strategic Malacca Strait. The British eventually emerged victorious. While they ruled their colony, known as Malaya, the British established the foundation of modern Malaysia's government and economy.

The Federation of Malaya gained its independence from Great Britain on August 31, 1957 (it was renamed the Federation of Malaysia in 1963). Since then the country has emerged as a powerful player in global economics and

A rickshaw is parked on a street in Penang. Life in Malaysia has been greatly influenced by centuries of trade with other cultures.

politics. During its early years of independence, Malaysia's economy was primarily based upon two commodities: rubber and tin. But during the first two decades after independence, Malaysia began a dramatic transformation from a producer of raw commodities to an industrialized country. By developing industries to process its natural resources, Malaysia diversified its economy, created numerous new jobs, and helped decrease poverty levels. This economic boom resulted in a high rural-to-urban migration as people left their farms and fishing villages to work in the cities.

Trade continues to play a vital role in the economy. Today the United States is Malaysia's largest trading partner and foreign investor; other traditional trading partners include Japan, the European Union, Australia, Singapore, and South Korea. Malaysia is also busily developing trade with other nations in Asia, Africa, Latin America, and the Middle East. The

Malaysia's former prime minister Mahathir bin Mohamad (second from right) smiles during a 2003 meeting with other government leaders in Cyberjaya to discuss the future of Malaysia's Multimedia Super Corridor. To strengthen the country's already-solid economy, in recent years Malaysia has focused on developing the information technology sector.

country's economy is highly dependent upon exports to global markets, and the government is continuously diversifying exports to suit global demand. Today, Malaysia is the 10th-largest trading nation in the world. During the past 30 years Malaysia's economy has sustained an average annual growth rate of 7 percent, and since 1963 the country's exports have grown from $1 billion to $100 billion. It currently counts over 134 states as its trading partners.

In its quest to become a fully industrialized nation by the year 2020, Malaysia in recent years has shifted its primary economic focus to the information technology (IT) sector. During the 1990s the government established the Multimedia Super Corridor (MSC), a commercial zone around Kuala Lumpur, Malaysia's capital. The primary architect of this vision was Dr. Mahathir bin Mohamad, who served as Malaysia's prime minister from 1981 to 2003. The MSC was created for a variety of objectives, including attracting important international investors, providing IT training in a variety of fields, and researching and developing future IT projects. At the core of the MSC is an ambitious plan to transform Malaysia into a world-class leader in global technology.

Today, Malaysians enjoy sustained economic growth, thanks to the country's large industrial base. The country's political system is much more democratic and open than the governments of many other Muslim countries. Malaysia also boasts one of the highest literacy rates in the Islamic world. Prosperity through unity lies at the core of Malaysia's harmonious progress, and the government fosters this concept through educational and political meetings that promote moderate religious beliefs. As a leading member of the Organization of the Islamic Conference (OIC), Malaysia has accepted a prominent role among Muslim countries. By almost any standard, Malaysia has become one of the most prosperous and successful nations in the Islamic world.

Stalactites hang from the roof of a large bat cave on the Malay Peninsula. Large limestone caves like this one can be found throughout the country.

2
The Land

Nestled between China and India, the nation of Malaysia occupies a strategic position in the heart of Southeast Asia. The country is composed of two geographical regions: Peninsular Malaysia, which occupies the southern portion of the Malay Peninsula, and East Malaysia, located on the island of Borneo about 400 miles (644 kilometers) across the South China Sea. The two regions, which make up an area slightly smaller than the U.S. state of New Mexico, are in turn divided into 13 states and 3 federal territories.

Both regions share certain geographical characteristics, such as sandy coastal plains that give way to mountainous interiors. Between the mountains and the plains lies the agricultural zone, where important crops like rice, rubber, and oil palm are grown. Malaysia is richly endowed with natural resources and possesses some of the world's largest tin deposits as well as large reserves of oil and natural gas. All of Malaysia's states have direct access to the sea, which remains a vital component in the nation's economy. Famed for its tropical beauty, Malaysia draws visitors from all over the world with its vast expanses of unspoiled rainforests, ancient cave systems, and scenic beaches.

Peninsular Malaysia

Eleven of the nation's thirteen states and two of its three federal territories are located in Peninsular Malaysia. This region, which comprises

The Geography of Malaysia

Location: Southeastern Asia, peninsula and northern one-third of the island of Borneo, bordering Indonesia and the South China Sea, south of Vietnam

Area: (slightly larger than New Mexico)
total: 127,316 square miles (329,750 sq km)
land: 126,853 square miles (328,550 sq km)
water: 463 square miles (1,200 sq km)

Borders: Brunei, 237 miles (381 km); Indonesia, 1,107 miles (1,782 km); Thailand, 314 miles (506 km)

Climate: tropical; annual southwest (April to October) and northeast (October to February) monsoons

Terrain: coastal plains rising to hills and mountains

Elevation extremes:
lowest point: Indian Ocean, 0 feet
highest point: Gunong Kinabalu, 13,451 feet (4,100 meters)

Natural hazards: flooding, landslides, forest fires

Source: Adapted from CIA World Factbook, 2009.

about 40 percent of the nation's total land area, is home to about 85 percent of the population. It also contains the federal territories of Kuala Lumpur (the official capital) and Putrajaya (the new administrative capital that has been undergoing construction since the mid-1990s).

Thailand borders Peninsular Malaysia to the north while the narrow Johor Strait separates the peninsula from the island nation of Singapore to the south. The South China Sea borders the peninsula to the east and the Malacca Strait, one of the busiest shipping lanes in the world, forms the nation's western boundary. This narrow strait is the main sea route between the Pacific and Indian Oceans and has played a vital role in Malaysia's history since ancient times.

East Malaysia

Sabah and Sarawak, the two states of East Malaysia, occupy the northern one-third of the island of Borneo. They share this island with the Indonesian territory of Kalimantan and the independent **sultanate** of Brunei.

The Malaysian federal territory of Labuan is a triangular-shaped island located about 6 miles (10 km) off the coast of Sabah. Its name is derived from the Malay word *labuhan*, meaning "anchorage," and aptly describes the deep, sheltered harbor that serves as the country's offshore financial center and duty-free port.

While East Malaysia is considerably less developed than Peninsular Malaysia, it holds most of the nation's natural resources, particularly its reserves of oil and natural gas. It also contains the world's oldest rainforests. These fragile ecosystems are teeming with unique wildlife and natural treasures.

Occupying an area of 48,050 square miles (124,150 sq km), Sarawak is the largest state in Malaysia, accounting for about 37.5 percent of the nation's total land area. The terrain of Sarawak consists of swampy coastlines that give way to a belt of gently rolling hills ringing the towering mountains of the interior. The forests of Sarawak, which cover over 67 percent of the land, are among the state's most valued resources, providing timber for export as well as a huge variety of forest products for domestic use.

Perched in the northeastern corner of Borneo, Sabah is the second-largest state in Malaysia. In ancient times it was known as the "Land Below the Wind" because it lies safely below the **typhoon** belt, an area that has the greatest frequency of typhoons in the world. The typhoon belt extends from southern Japan to the central Philippines to eastern Micronesia.

Limestone caves can be found all over Malaysia, but the largest and most famous caves are found in Sarawak at Mulu National Park. Clearwater Cave is the longest cave in Southeast Asia and the tenth longest in the world, with a 66-mile (107-km) passageway. Sarawak Chamber, which measures 1,968 feet (600 meters) long by 1,361 feet (415 meters) wide and has a ceiling span of 984 feet (300 meters), is the largest subterranean chamber in the world. It is big enough to hold 40 jumbo jets and even the most powerful lanterns cannot penetrate the darkness from wall to wall or from floor to ceiling. The caves of Mulu National Park draw visitors from all over the world.

Mountains

The Banjaran Titiwangsa, or "Main Range," forms the mountainous spine of Peninsular Malaysia. Running from the Thai border in the north to the state of Negeri Sembilan in southern Malaysia, the range divides the country roughly in half, separating the eastern and western regions of the peninsula. In ancient times it took about a month to cross the Main Range astride an elephant. Today the East-West Highway, which opened in 1983, weaves through the mountains.

The highest peak in Peninsular Malaysia is Gunong Tahan (*gunong* means "mountain" in Malay). Located in the central state of Pahang and within the Main Range, Gunong Tahan rises 7,186 feet (2,190 meters) above sea level.

However, the highest peak in Malaysia is nearly twice as high as Gunong Tahan. Gunong Kinabalu, which dominates the rugged and densely forested terrain of Sabah, rises 13,451 feet (4,100 meters) high, making it the highest mountain in Southeast Asia. The mist-shrouded mountain is very special to the people of Sabah and plays a major role in the cultural traditions of the region. The Kadazan-Dusun people, the

Mountains rise behind the lush growth of a banana plantation.

state's largest native tribe, believe the mountain is home to the departed souls of their ancestors. The name *Kinabalu* is believed to stem from a local Dusunic term meaning "sacred dwelling of the dead." Many visitors arrive each year to climb to the summit, an adventurous undertaking that usually takes several days. Those who reach the summit are rewarded with an eye-popping panorama of Borneo and the South China Sea.

Bodies of Water

Rivers have been the lifeblood of Malaysia since ancient times. They are a vital source of transportation, communication, and trade. As evidence of how historically important these bodies of water are, nearly all the states in Peninsular Malaysia derive their names from the principal rivers that flow through them.

The 285-mile-long (459-km-long) Pahang River is the longest river in Peninsular Malaysia. Much of the state of Pahang lies in the river basin. The people of this densely forested region depend on the river for transportation as well as irrigation. Plantations and smaller farms along the riverbanks produce such important commercial crops as rubber, palm oil, coconuts, tobacco, rattan, and hemp. Although the river is beneficial to the people, it can also be dangerous. During the northeast monsoon season it can rise dramatically, and deforestation along the riverbanks has contributed to heavy flooding in some areas.

Sarawak, which has been called the "Land of Many Rivers," is home to the 398-mile-long (641-km-long) Rajang River (also spelled *Rejang*), the longest river and busiest waterway in Malaysia. This mighty river is a major transportation and communication link between the coastal and interior regions. The Rajang and its major tributaries—the Baleh, Balui, Belaga, Murum, and Linau—flow west from the highlands in eastern Sarawak, irrigating 15,444 square miles (40,000 sq km) of land before pouring into the South China Sea. Another major waterway is the 250-mile

The Salak River winds its way through coastal mangrove swamps and forests in Sarawak. In the background, Mount Santubong rises from the sea.

long (400-km-long) Baram River, which flows northwest into the South China Sea.

The Kinabatangan River is Sabah's longest river, and the second-longest in Malaysia. As the 348-mile-long (560-km-long) river reaches the lowlands it meanders over a vast floodplain of *oxbow lakes* and marshlands, creating an ecosystem that is home to one of the largest and most varied concentrations of wildlife in the world. The most commonly used watercraft in Sabah is the *perahu*, a low-slung, pencil-thin wooden canoe equipped with an outboard motor. This surprisingly fast and agile craft passes nonchalantly over churning whitewater rapids and is often used to transport people and goods between coastal towns.

The construction of dams on some of Malaysia's rivers has created many lakes. Kenyir Lake, located in the state of Terengganu, was formed when a hydroelectric dam was built on the Kenyir River. This created the

A small but sturdy *perahu* is beached on Penang. Small boats like this, equipped with outboard motors, are commonly used to transport people and goods up and down the rivers of Malaysia.

largest manmade lake in Southeast Asia, covering an area of 142 square miles (369 sq km). The lake contains about 340 small islands (these were once hilltops before the area was flooded). Because of its location near the entrance to Malaysia National Park it has become a popular tourist destination.

Climate

Malaysia is located just a few degrees above the equator, so its climate is tropical and wet all year round, averaging 80 to 90 percent relative humidity. Daytime temperatures are always warm but not usually extremely high, and nights are fairly cool. Average daytime temperatures in Kuala Lumpur range between 72° and 90° Fahrenheit (22° and 32° Celsius), while daytime temperatures in the highlands average around 55°

to 80°F (13° to 27°C). Temperatures at the peak of Gunong Kinabalu may drop to near freezing, particularly at night.

Malaysians must take rainy days in stride, because it rains from 150 to 200 days a year. Sudden heavy downpours are common. Total annual rainfall averages about 100 inches (254 cm) in Peninsular Malaysia and 150 inches (381 cm) in East Malaysia. Some regions, particularly the exposed northern slopes of East Malaysia, regularly record an average of 200 inches (508 cm) of rain per year.

Malaysia has two main seasons, although the transitions between these seasons are not usually well defined. The seasons are not marked by changing temperatures, but by changes in wind flow directions. In general, the northeast monsoon season runs from October to February, and the southwest monsoon season occurs from April to October.

Flora and Fauna

The forests of Malaysia, which cover more than 58 percent of the land, contain many species of valuable hardwood trees as well as a stunning variety of plants and animals. Malaysia is considered one of the world's 12 **biodiversity hotspots** and provides a home to many endangered species. For example, the endangered leatherback turtle can be spotted on the tiny beach of Rantau Abang on Terengganu's scenic coast. The beach is one of only six places in the world where people can watch these rare turtles lay their eggs, which they do between May and September every year.

Malaysia's rich plant and animal life includes 14,500 different flowering plants and trees, and more than 280 types of mammals, 600 bird species, 350 types of reptiles, 165 different amphibians, and thousands of unique insect and invertebrate species. More than 2,000 of Malaysia's plant and animal species are native to the country and cannot be found anywhere else in the world.

Fifteen different kinds of forest thrive in Malaysia, each with its own unique ecosystem. In addition to providing vital habitats for wildlife, the forests also hold much potential for medicinal cures. For example, a drug derived from the leaves of the bintangor tree, which can be found only in the swampy lowlands of Sarawak, is currently being tested as a potential treatment for AIDS. There may be many other beneficial substances in the rainforest that no one knows about yet. Currently about one-quarter of all Western pharmaceuticals are derived from rainforest plants, but the medicinal possibilities of only about 1 percent of these valuable tropical plants have been fully researched. Unfortunately, the world's rainforests are diminishing rapidly due to logging and the expansion of human settlements, so many potential cures may be lost before the rainforests can be fully explored.

A huge variety of trees flourish in the forests of Malaysia, including 200 species of palms. One unusual tree is the tualang, which grows in solitary splendor in damp locations along the Malaysian lowlands. Tualang trees are the third-tallest species in the world and can reach heights of 250 feet (76 meters). The tualang's wood is so hard it is nearly impossible to cut, so it is almost never used for timber. Instead, the towering tree is prized for the honey it provides. As the preferred home of the one-inch-long Asian rock bee (the largest honeybee in the world), the trees are often draped with immense disk-shaped honeycombs, some of which can measure over 6 feet (2 meters) across. Nearly 1,000 pounds (454 kilograms) of honey can be gathered from the colossal honeycombs of one tree. Other valuable trees include the fast-growing teak, the richly hued mahogany, and the gaharu, a prized source of aromatic resins for making incense.

Malaysia's exotic flowers include more than 3,000 varieties of wild orchids, the hibiscus (Malaysia's national flower), the bird of paradise, and the rafflesia, the world's largest flower. The rare and ***parasitic*** rafflesia (also called the corpse lily) grows wild in Sabah and Sarawak, and has

> Rainforests are home to half of the world's plant and animal species. Malaysia contains the grandfather of all rainforests, older than those of the Amazon or the Congo. Malaysia's hot climate kept the rain forests warm enough for life to develop, even during ice ages 130 million years ago when glaciers covered much of the earth.

three-foot-wide blooms weighing up to 20 pounds (9 kg) that smell like rotting meat to attract insects. The plant only blooms once a year and the putrid flowers only live for about a week. Also found in East Malaysia is the largest of the pitcher plants (*Nepenthes rajah*), which can hold up to a half-gallon of water, effectively trapping insects that stop for a sip.

Malaysia is home to many endangered or threatened animals. The endangered Asian elephant (sometimes called the Indian elephant) and the Malayan elephant (a subspecies of the Asian elephant) can be found in small herds in protected sanctuaries and national parks throughout the country. Currently, the number of wild elephants roaming the forests of Malaysia is estimated at from 2,300 to 3,000.

In 2003 the Sabah Wildlife Department made an exciting discovery. Through DNA sampling they confirmed a new subspecies of the Asian elephant—the Borneo pygmy elephant. Research performed at Columbia University proved that the Borneo elephants were isolated from their cousins on Asia and Sumatra about 300,000 years ago. They developed unique genetic distinctions such as smaller size, larger ears, and relatively straight tusks. Today, the research continues and preserving the Borneo pygmy elephants has become a high conservation priority.

Malaysia's forests are home to eight species of wild cats. The Malayan tiger (also called the Indochinese tiger) is the national animal of Malaysia. The elusive tiger, which can measure over 8 feet (2.5 meters) long and

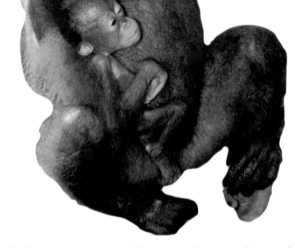

weigh over 330 pounds (150 kg), is the largest predator in the country. Other big cats of Malaysia include the clouded leopard, the golden cat, the panther, the marbled cat, the leopard cat, the flat-headed cat, and the bay cat. Tigers, panthers, and golden cats are found only in Peninsular Malaysia while the bay cat lives only in East Malaysia.

Other Malaysian mammals include the endangered tapirs and Sumatran rhinoceroses; several species of wild cattle; and a variety of wild deer, including the lesser mouse deer, the smallest hoofed mammal in the world. Malaysia's seven species of primates include orangutans and three species of protected gibbons (fruit-eating, long-armed apes). The

A baby orangutan clings to his mother while she dangles from a branch in the Sepilok Orangutan Sanctuary in Sabah.

Kinabatangan Wildlife Sanctuary in Sabah is one of only two places in the world where 10 species of primates live in the same area. The endangered orangutan (this name derives from the Malay orang hutan, meaning "man of the forest") lives only in Borneo and Sumatra. These highly intelligent primates can be found roaming freely in the Kinabatangan Wildlife Sanctuary and the Sepilok Orangutan Sanctuary.

Bats account for about 40 percent of all mammals in Malaysia. They share the skies with a huge variety of birds, including hornbills, parrots, eagles, hawks, owls, herons, storks, egrets, ducks, geese, and swiflets, whose edible nests are internationally prized as delicacies. Malaysia's reptiles and amphibians include the king cobra, which is the largest venomous snake in the world; the reticulated python (the world's second-largest snake); the freshwater terrapin; the monitor lizard; the crocodile; and a huge variety of frogs and lizards. Malaysia's insect population is particularly diverse, boasting 1,000 species of butterflies alone.

The waters of Malaysia are similarly rich with marine life, including over 100 species of carp as well as the giant catfish (*ikan tapah*), which can grow up to nearly six feet (two meters) long and weigh nearly 100 pounds (45 kg).

Today the vast rainforests of Malaysia are under threat due to agricultural clearing, mining, logging, industrial waste, pollution, and natural forest fires and landslides. A variety of conservation groups, including Malaysia's Department of Environment, the Sabah Wildlife Department, Sarawak's Wildlife Division, and the World Wildlife Fund are hard at work researching and preserving the country's natural treasures.

Malaysians light candles and pray during a special inter-religious service for victims of a deadly tsunami that pounded the Indian Ocean in December 2004. Malaysia was not hit as hard as some of its neighbors, such as Indonesia, but the tsunami did displace more than 8,000 Malaysians living in coastal areas.

3

The History

The abundant plant and animal life in Malaysia made the region a desirable place for prehistoric peoples to settle. However, trade ultimately shaped much of Malaysia's history as well as its ethnic composition. Since ancient times, traders from China, India, the Middle East, Indonesia, and Thailand flocked to the Malay Archipelago. Ethnic Malays, who are descended from a combination of these ethnic groups, are called *bumiputeras*, a Sanskrit term meaning "princes of the earth."

First Peoples

A number of archeological discoveries have revealed clues about the earliest inhabitants of Malaysia. Two of the most important archeological sites in Malaysia are the Lenggong Valley in Perak and the Mulu Caves in Sarawak. Through evidence such as skeletal remains, tools, and cave drawings, most researchers agree that the first human residents of present-day Malaysia were the Semang peoples of Peninsular Malaysia and the Dayak peoples of Sabah and Sarawak. These two groups still live among the Malaysian population today.

The ancestors of the Semang were the Orang Asli, an Asian group to which the Semang belong. They are believed to have been among the first wave of settlers migrating southward on an overland route from China and Tibet around 98,000 B.C. By 38,000 B.C., the ancestors of the present-day Dayak peoples of East Malaysia had settled in the Mulu Caves in Sarawak. The Dayak were **Austronesian** peoples who came by sea, most likely from mainland Asia and the islands between the two regions.

The next group of settlers to arrive in Malaysia was the Proto-Malays, who came from China around 3000 B.C. They were accomplished seafarers and farmers, and brought the important skill of metalworking with them. The Proto-Malays settled in the coastal areas of the peninsula, East Malaysia, and on the islands between the two regions. Around 300 B.C. the Malaysia region was flooded with immigrants, as settlers arrived from India, the Middle East, China, Indonesia, Thailand, and other neighboring regions. Members of these ethnic groups, along with the Proto-Malays, were the ancestors of the present-day Malay people. During the next century these newcomers established strong trading links with China, India, and the Middle East, and played a major role in shaping the first great Malay empires.

Early Malay Kingdoms

Around the first century A.D., events in China and India would set the course for Malaysia to become a bustling center of international trade. Kingdoms in India had established a lucrative trade with the vast Roman Empire, which controlled the Mediterranean region. However, the overland trade route between India and Rome was cut off by the Huns, a nomadic tribe of invaders from western China. To make matters worse, the Roman emperor Vespasian, who ruled from A.D. 69 to 79, stopped the empire's shipments of gold to India. At that point, Indians took to the sea in quest of alternate trade routes and dependable sources of gold.

Early Indian scholars wrote of a mystical place in the eastern isles called Suvarnadvipa (Land of Gold), and it was the quest for gold that lured Indian traders to the Malay Peninsula. Following the monsoon winds, the traders arrived on the western coast, in the present-day state of Kedah, around A.D. 100. These early explorers did not find any gold, but they did find bountiful deposits of tin. This important mineral, used in making bronze, quickly became a valuable trading resource. Around the same time Chinese traders, who also were seeking to increase trade, arrived to forge relations with the small Malay kingdoms established on the peninsula.

In addition to bringing Malaysians goods for barter, the traders brought their religious beliefs, culture, and philosophies of government. The religions of Hinduism and Buddhism spread quickly throughout the region.

For centuries Malaysia has been a center of trade between China, India, and other Asian cultures. This porcelain bottle, shaped like a dog and made during China's Ming dynasty, was found in a shipwreck off Kuala Dungun in Malaysia's northern state of Terengganu.

The ancient Malay kings were particularly impressed with India's efficient form of government. They combined Indian traditions—such as the ruler title of **raja** (prince)—with their own customs, creating what historians call "Indianized states." Today, numerous temple sites still stand as reminders of the Hindu-Buddhist period.

In the centuries that followed, maritime trade flourished and the region continued to grow as a center of commerce. However, rivalries among neighboring kingdoms also grew as the Indianized states of the Malay Peninsula, as well as on Sumatra and Java (both islands are part of present-day Indonesia), sought to control larger shares of the commercial traffic passing through the Malacca Strait. Several powerful empires, including Srivijaya (a Hindu-Buddhist kingdom located across the strait in Sumatra) and Majapahit (a Hindu kingdom based in Java), rose and fell. During the late 1300s, the Srivijayan prince Parameswara was forced to flee his kingdom in Sumatra. He eventually resettled in Melaka, beginning a chain of events in which the dominant religion of the Malay archipelago was transformed from Hinduism to Islam.

Islam and the Sultanate of Melaka

According to the time-honored account of Malay history known as the *Sejarah Melayu* (or *Malay Annals),* Parameswara and his band of royal refugees first settled in Melaka around 1400. Strategically located along the Malacca Strait, the city started as a small fishing village but within a few years developed into a rich and powerful center of maritime trade. In 1403, the first official trade envoy from China, led by Admiral Yin Ching, arrived in what was now the sultanate of Melaka. Six years later Admiral Zheng He, commander of the Chinese imperial fleet, paid his first visit to the city. Trade between Melaka and China flourished and many Chinese traders settled in the region, bringing about a vibrant blend of Malay and Chinese culture. From this cultural exchange emerged a distinct ethnic

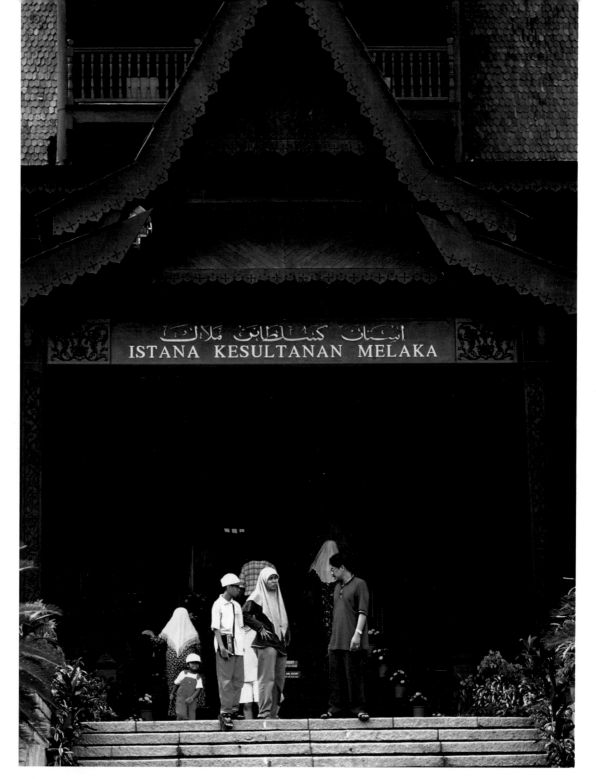

استان کسلطانن ملاک

ISTANA KESULTANAN MELAKA

This is a modern reconstruction of the *istana*, or palace, of Sultan Mansur Shah, a ruler of Melaka around 1465. Melaka emerged as a powerful Muslim kingdom during the 15th century.

group, the Baba-Nyonya (once also known as the Straits Chinese). Numerous Indian traders also settled along the strait during this time, bringing the message of Islam with them.

After Parameswara married an Indonesian Muslim princess in 1414, the prince embraced Islam and changed his name to Raja Iskandar Shah. The people of Melaka quickly followed his lead and converted to Islam. By this time, Islam had also spread to the coastal areas of Borneo. One reason Islam spread so rapidly throughout the region was that the Qur'an, the scripture that included the religion's basic teachings, prohibited class discrimination. Unlike the Hindu caste system, in which people could never move above the level of society into which they had been born, Islam provided an opportunity for smart or ambitious people to advance themselves. In the Muslim community, people were supposed to be judged on their individual merits, rather than their social class.

As Islam spread throughout the region more Muslim traders arrived in Melaka, bringing the city international fame. At its peak, Melaka was the most important port in the East. Hundreds of trading ships docked in the harbor each year bringing silks, porcelain, and tea from China; textiles from India; sandalwood from Timor; spices from Java; and gold and pepper from Sumatra. Over 80 different languages were spoken in the city, and special housing was built to accommodate traders from different cultural backgrounds. To facilitate trade, the rulers of Melaka instituted a variety of innovative measures. For example, the sultanate's fleet was organized to protect trading vessels and escort them safely into port, and the Syahbandar (Port Authority) took care of traders' business needs, providing bilingual translators so that they could deal with merchants from other parts of the world and providing storehouses for their wares.

For over a century, the sultans of Melaka ruled both sides of the strait, marking the classical era of Malay culture. However, prosperity had its price. During the late 1400s, the bustling port attracted the attention of

European rulers who sought to gain control over trade with the East in order to enrich their own countries.

The Colonial Era

Spices, silks, and other valuable and exotic goods from Asia had been reintroduced to Europe during the period of the Crusades (1096–1291), a series of religious wars fought between Christians and Muslims for control over Jerusalem and the surrounding "Holy Land." The goods were brought from China and India to Europe via the Silk Road, an ancient network of trade routes that crossed Central Asia. However, the people of Europe had to pay high prices for the goods because of the danger and time involved in traversing this long route. Also, the Muslim traders who brought the goods to European ports could charge high prices, because Europeans were not permitted to dock at ports along the Arabian Peninsula.

During the 15th century, the small kingdom of Portugal on the Iberian Peninsula began to send ships to explore south along the coast of Africa. One goal of these voyages was to find a passage around Africa that would enable Portuguese traders to sail directly to ports in Asia, bypassing the Arab middlemen. This would give Portugal access to spices and other goods at cheaper prices. In 1497–99, the voyage of Vasco da Gama brought to fruition nearly 80 years of Portuguese exploration. The Portuguese navigator commanded a small fleet that rounded the southern tip of Africa, landed at several ports in the Indian Ocean, and returned to Portugal with a load of valuable goods.

Gama's first voyage had been relatively peaceful, but the Arabs attacked subsequent Portuguese voyages in an attempt to preserve their trade monopoly. To protect Portugese shipping, warships were sent to conquer strategic ports and establish Portugal's control over the lucrative Indian Ocean trade. In 1511, a Portuguese fleet led by Alfonso de Albuquerque captured Melaka, ushering in an era of colonialism that

Portuguese ships destroy an Arab dhow in the Indian Ocean. When the Portuguese arrived in the 16th century, their warships were armed with cannons, a weapon previously unknown to the Muslims of the region. This gave them a military advantage that enabled the Europeans to capture Melaka and other important Indian Ocean seaports.

would last until the mid-20th century. Soon after raising their flag in Melaka, the Portuguese constructed a massive stone fortress called A Fomasa, from which they could control their trade monopoly.

Thanks to its network of African and Asian trading posts, Portugal soon became the wealthiest nation in Europe. However, other countries wanted a share of the Asian sea trade, and Portugal quickly found itself besieged by competing European powers. The Portuguese had to fight almost constantly to maintain their hold over the region. In 1606, the

Dutch East Indies Company, a trading corporation chartered by the Netherlands, made a formal pact with the sultan of Johor, a kingdom at the southern tip of the Malay Peninsula. The sultan was descended from the family that had ruled Melaka before the Portuguese arrived. The treaty stipulated that if the Dutch ousted the Portuguese from Melaka, the sultan would permit the Dutch to keep the city and conduct trade in Johor. In addition, both parties agreed to respect one another's religious beliefs; this would be a welcome change for the Muslim Malays, who had endured nearly a century of religious persecution under the Christian Portuguese. After several failed attempts and lengthy sieges, the Dutch and their allies from Johor succeeded in capturing Melaka in 1641.

By the mid-1700s, Britain's East India Company had joined the trading frenzy centered around the Malay Peninsula, and was carrying on a lively trade with India. However, the British lacked a safe port where they could dock their ships and take on provisions on the way to and from India. They resented the heavy taxes imposed upon British ships that docked in Dutch ports in the Indian Ocean. In 1786, Sir Francis Light of the British East India Company convinced the sultan of Kedah to give up possession of Penang Island in exchange for British protection and financial compensation. The British now had a foothold in the region and built a settlement called Georgetown, which gave them a safe and accessible port from which to conduct trade.

When France conquered the Netherlands in 1795, the Emperor Napoleon claimed all Dutch territories, including its possessions on the Malay Peninsula. However, the exiled Dutch government in Melaka had no desire to give its French enemies the prosperous city. Aware that the British—France's economic and military rival—were anxious to protect their own trading interests in Asia, the Dutch allowed Great Britain to take temporary possession of Melaka. This marked the start of Britain's expansion into the Malay Peninsula, which it would eventually control. By 1826

Britain had consolidated its East India Company holdings, which included Penang Island, Singapore, and Melaka, into a British colony called the Straits Settlements. When the British East India Company was dissolved in the mid-1800s, the British government took over the administration of the Straits Settlements. In 1867, the territory was proclaimed a crown colony.

During the next several decades, the colonial government rapidly developed what it called British Malaya by expanding the tin mining industry, establishing rubber plantations, and constructing roads and railways to transport these goods to the colony's ports. The British brought Chinese laborers to work in the mines and Indians to work in the rubber plantations, while they encouraged the native Malays to farm for a living in order to the feed the growing workforce. Workers constructed the first roadways connecting the rapidly growing urban centers of Kuala Lumpur and Johor Baharu, and laid the first railway tracks from the city of Taiping, in Perak (once the richest tin-mining region in the world), to Port Weld (Perak's transportation hub at the time). The British also ordered the construction of a telegraph network and a postal system.

Despite these modern developments, the people of Malaya were overworked and underpaid, and they chafed under colonial rule. To prevent the local population from uniting against them, the British ensured division among the Malay, Chinese, and Indian communities by governing each of them separately.

While the British assumed control over the Straits Settlements, they gradually expanded their authority in other parts of modern-day Malaysia. During the 1830s, for example, some native peoples of what is now East Malaysia rebelled against the ruling Sultan of Brunei. The Malay governor of Sarawak, Raja Muda Hashim, turned to British adventurer James Brooke for assistance in quelling the rebellion. Brooke had arrived in 1839, commanding a well-armed schooner. For his help in putting down the resistance, in 1841 the raja invited Brooke to govern Sarawak. The Brooke family, known as the "White Rajas," ruled benevolently for over a century. In contrast to how most colonial rulers governed, the White Rajas protected the indigenous peoples from exploitation as they expanded and developed their territory. They also encouraged ethnic harmony by inviting the local Malays and Muslims to help govern the state. Sarawak's neighbor state, Sabah, was taken over in 1881 by the British North Borneo Company and was declared a **protectorate** of Britain.

By 1919, the British had either direct sovereignty or colonial control over all the lands of present-day Malaysia. As developments in agriculture, industry, communications, and transportation grew, the Straits Settlements drew many immigrants from nearby regions. In 1850, the colony's population had been less than 500,000 people. By 1932, the population had swelled to nearly 4 million, and the agricultural sector had made the transition from **subsistence** farming to growing cash crops such as sugarcane, coffee, and rubber.

The Creation of Malaysia

By the 1930s, Japan had become the most modernized nation in Asia. But to gain raw goods for manufacturing and firmly

British army officer and explorer James Brooke (1803–1868) became the raja of Sarawak after helping the ruler put down a rebellion. His family ruled Sarawak until it officially became a British colony in 1946.

establish itself as the dominant power in the Pacific, Japan needed to control the natural resources of the Malay Archipelago. Just days after attacking the U.S. naval base at Pearl Harbor in December 1941, Japanese forces landed in British Malaya. By March 1942, Japan had captured most of Malaya, as well as the British colonies in Singapore and North Borneo and the Dutch colonies in other parts of the archipelago.

Immediately after the Pearl Harbor attack the United States declared war on Japan, entering World War II. The United States formed an alliance with Britain and other countries, and focused on defeating Germany in Europe and Africa while also pushing the Japanese out of the Pacific islands they had occupied. After Japan surrendered to the Allies in August 1945, Britain once again resumed control over Malaya.

Both Sarawak and Sabah formally ceded their sovereignty to the British Crown in 1946, and in 1948 the British created the Federation of Malaya, which included all 11 states in Peninsular Malaysia. However, by this time a large number of Malay **communists** had fled to the jungles, where they established an armed resistance opposed to continued British colonial rule. (Ironically, many of the insurgents had been armed and trained by the British during World War II to harass Japanese forces.) The Malayan Communist Party (MCP), a predominantly Chinese group that had been formed in 1930, wanted to reclaim Malaya from the British and make it a communist state. Led by Chin Peng, the MCP received support from the many Malay Chinese who had been denied land rights and suffered economical hardships under British rule. On June 16, 1948, the MCP executed three British rubber planters, pushing the British government to declare a state of emergency in the colony.

What became known as the Malayan Emergency lasted for 12 years. Travel throughout the country became both difficult and dangerous as the MCP launched a campaign of terror that destroyed roads, railways, and government installations. As a result, economic conditions worsened.

Malay police raid a suspected meeting of communist guerillas, July 1948. The Malayan Emergency, during which the British and Malay governments battled a communist insurgency, lasted until 1960.

During this time, the British moved Malaysians of Chinese descent from their remote villages into new communities. The purpose of these so-called New Villages was to protect villagers from the communists, who often emerged from the jungles to demand food or money, as well as to isolate any potential communist supporters in the population. Deprived of their source of supplies and information, the MCP began attacking the new settlements. The insurgents continued to put up a fight, but were finally defeated in 1960.

Although the general population did not support the communist rebellion, between 1948 and 1960 a movement for an independent Malaysia slowly gained popular support. After World War II ended, three major political parties emerged in British Malaya: the United Malays National Organization (UMNO), the Malayan Chinese Association (MCA), and the Malayan Indian Congress (MIC). In 1951 Tunku (Prince) Abdul Rahman (1903–1990) was elected president of the UMNO. Tunku, as he was affectionately known, immediately began promoting national unity by traveling all over the country and meeting people from all walks of life. His successful efforts resulted in the creation of the Alliance Party, a multi-ethnic political coalition that included the UMNO, the MCA, and the MIC. Under Tunku's leadership the Alliance Party won an overwhelming victory in the colony's first general elections, held in 1955, and Tunku was appointed chief minister and minister of home affairs. Shortly afterward, Tunku traveled to London to discuss Malaya's independence with British leaders. On August 31, 1957, the Federation of Malaya became an independent nation. Tunku was selected as Malaya's first prime minister and served in that position from 1957 to 1970.

In 1961 Tunku invited Singapore, Sarawak, Sabah, and Brunei to join the independent federation. All but Brunei joined the federation in 1963, although Singapore peacefully withdrew in 1965 due to racial, economic, and political disputes. The new federation was renamed Malaysia on September 16, 1963.

Malaysia's early years were marked by strife, as both Indonesia and the Philippines claimed parts of East Malaysia and threatened to take them by force. When Sarawak joined the federation, Indonesia's President Sukarno feared that the new union would eventually encroach upon his

Tunku Abdul Rahman (second from right) signs the final document of the Federation of Malaya Constitutional Conference at Lancaster House in London, February 1956. Watching him is the secretary of state for the colonies, Alan Lennox Boyd. Malaysia officially became independent in August 1957.

territory. He angrily denounced the federation as a British puppet, promised to "crush Malaysia," and launched an armed resistance. The conflict, known as the Confrontation, lasted for several years as Indonesian and communist guerillas fought against Malaysian, British, and Australian forces in Sarawak. It finally ended when Sukarno was stripped of power in 1965–66 after a coup by General Suharto. In addition, the Philippines claim Sabah, although they have not pressed this claim for many years.

Despite Tunku's efforts at uniting the various ethnic groups of Malaysia, racial tension dominated the nation's politics for many years.

The Malaysian national anthem, *Negara ku* ("My Country"), is an adaptation of the Perak State Anthem, and was chosen for its traditional melody and sentiment. Any disrespect towards the national anthem is a criminal offense and the honor of performing it is restricted.

The Malays, collectively called *bumiputeras*, were the largest segment of the population, but ethnic Chinese controlled the greatest share of the country's economy. At the time, the *bumiputeras* made up 50 percent of the population but earned only about 2.5 percent of the national income, compared to over 30 percent earned by the ethnic Chinese.

Tensions over this economic imbalance erupted into violence between Malays and Chinese following the 1969 general elections, in which the Chinese-dominated Democratic Action Party (DAP) gained a large number of seats from the Malay-dominated Alliance Party. Bloody race riots in Kuala Lumpur claimed the lives of at least 200 people. The country was in a state of emergency for two years, during which the government suspended the assembly, curtailed freedom of the press, and created the National Operations Council to serve as an interim governing body. Tunku stepped down as prime minister in September 1970; he was succeeded by Tun Abdul Razak, who promised to address the economic and social inequalities that fueled racial resentment.

Parliament finally reconvened in February 1971. The following year it passed the New Economic Policy (NEP), which was designed to level the nation's economic imbalance. The NEP gave *bumiputeras* a variety of special legal and economic privileges, including preference in housing, admission to college, positions in government, and ownership in business. A goal of the NEP was to reduce both poverty and identification of ecomomic function with race. Although many Malaysians (as well as much of the international community) view this policy as racial discrimination, it has been written into the Malaysian constitution. (However, in recent years the Malaysian government has discussed phasing out these advantages in favor of a system of **meritocracy.**)

Modern History

Since the turbulent decades following its independence, Malaysia has generally maintained a delicate balance between ethnicity, religion, and politics. This balance, and government stability, enabled it to focus on economic development. Under the leadership of Abdul Razak (1970–1976) and Tun Hussein Onn (1976–1981), some of the groundwork was laid for Malaysia to become an exporter of finished goods. However, it was after Dr. Mahathir bin Mohamad took over as prime minister in 1981 that Malaysia's economy really took off.

Mahathir wanted Malaysia to stand on its own without a need for foreign involvement. Although his government permitted foreign investment in Malaysia's economy, under the New Economic Policy Mahathir made sure that Malaysians gained ownership of the nation's businesses and industries. He also reformed the tax structure, reduced tariffs, and privatized various state-owned enterprises. Politically, under Mahathir's leadership the ruling party Barisan Nasional (National Front), a coalition that had replaced the Alliance Party in 1973, won landslide victories in the 1982, 1986, 1990, 1995, and 1999 general elections.

This political and economic stability created a climate in which the economy could prosper. By the mid-1990s, Malaysia had one of the strongest economies in Southeast Asia. As the manufacturing sector grew, many Malaysians were added to a prosperous and growing middle class. Although Malaysia faced severe setbacks during the 1997–98 Asian financial crisis, the national economy remained resilient. Many Malaysians attribute this success to Prime Minister Mohamad's economic incentives.

A survivor of the 2004 tsunami shows Malaysian prime minister Abdullah Ahmad Badawi (third from right) the height of the wave that battered his house in Permatang Damar Laut, a village in Penang.

During the early 1990s, Mahathir created a project called Vision 2020, which included heavy spending in the technology sector. The project was designed to spur Malaysia into attaining developed industrialized nation status by the year 2020.

However, Mahathir was not without his critics. Many observers considered him an obstacle to true democracy, citing his authoritarian leadership style. The prime minister stifled dissent by closing newspapers and arresting opposition leaders. Mahathir passed strict laws which he said were to protect the country from radical Islamist terrorism and ethnic strife. Opponents argued that these laws, which permit the government to detain suspects without formally charging them with crimes or requiring them to be placed on trial, have been used against political opponents.

In October 2003, Mahathir retired, and was succeeded by Abdullah bin Ahmad Badawi. As prime minister, Badawi focused on reducing government corruption. His administration arrested several public figures from the Mahathir era for corruption; this move received widespread public support. After implementing many reforms during his first year in office, the ruling National Front coalition won 90 percent of parliamentary seats in March 2004 elections and Abdullah was reelected.

During his term Badawi moved away from the economic policies of his predecessor. His Ninth Malaysia Plan, unveiled in 2006, called for privatization of some industries, increased government spending on infrastructure development, and improvements to agriculture in Malaysia. Additionally, in late 2005 Malaysia entered a historic free-trade agreement with Japan in which the two countries agreed to eliminate tariffs on many goods and products over a decade.

In April 2009, Badawi resigned as prime minister and as president of UMNO. His deputy, Najib Razak, was sworn in as the nation's new prime minister on April 3, 2009.

Trains enter and depart from a light rail transit station in Kuala Lumpur. Over the past 40 years, the government of Malaysia has invested heavily in the country's infrastructure so that the country's economy will continue to grow.

4

Politics, Religion, and the Economy

In many ways, Malaysia's government is different from that of the United States. Malaysia has a parliamentary system, with a constitutional monarchy. All Malaysian citizens who are at least 21 years old are allowed to vote in general elections, held every five years. They elect representatives to their state assemblies, as well as to the national parliament, a bicameral assembly, from which national leaders are selected.

The sultans of the states that make up the Federation of Malaysia, who inherit their titles, still play a role in politics. The king of Malaysia (called

Yang di-Pertuan Agong, or "Paramount Ruler") is the ceremonial head of state while the prime minister, selected from the lower house of parliament, is the country's chief executive. Sultan Tuanku Mizan Zainal Abidin of Terengganu was installed as Malaysia's 13th king in December 2006.

Unlike the United States and most other Western countries, Malaysia does not separate religion and politics. Malaysia is a Muslim nation and Islam plays a major role in its national and foreign policies. While Chinese and Indian Malaysians and other minority groups have the freedom to choose what religion to practice, by law ethnic Malays must practice Islam.

Government in Malaysia

Nine of Malaysia's states are ruled by Muslim sultans (the other four states—Melaka, Penang, Sabah, and Sarawak—have governors to perform the same function). Every five years the nine sultans—collectively called the Council of Rulers—elect one of their own to serve as Malaysia's king. Each sultan is allowed to serve as king only once in his lifetime. The king, who works closely with the prime minister, is responsible for upholding the customs and traditions of the Malay people and is the religious leader of the nation.

Although theoretically the king holds executive power, it is chiefly a ceremonial position. Malaysia's constitution specifies that control over day-to-day government operations rests with the cabinet, which is led by the prime minister. The prime minister is the leader of the party that holds the most seats in the legislature after every election cycle. (Historically, this has meant the leader of UMNO also serves as prime minister.) Malaysia's cabinet is composed of numerous ministries that oversee various areas of government, such as agriculture, education, finance, and defense.

Malaysia's king, Sultan Tuanku Mizan Zainal Abidin (center), salutes during a June 2008 parade in Kuala Lumpur to honor his birthday. The Muslim sultans that rule nine of Malaysia's states select the king from among their number.

Federal laws are written and approved by Malaysia's parliament, which is made up of two assemblies: Dewan Negara ("Hall of the Nation," which corresponds to the Senate in the U.S. Congress) and Dewan Rakyat ("Hall of the People," similar to the U.S. House of Representatives). There are 70 members of Dewan Negara, who serve six-year terms; the assemblies of each of Malaysia's 13 states elect two members, for a total of 26, while the remaining 44 are appointed by the king. All 193 members of Dewan Rakyat are selected by the people during the general elections and serve five-year terms. In Malaysia, a bill becomes a law only after it has been passed by both houses of Parliament.

Malaysia's judicial system is based upon English common law. Its primary function is to uphold the Constitution (the supreme law of the land), enforce the laws of the nation, and dispense justice. The court structure includes the Federal Court, Court of Appeal, High Court of Malaya (in Peninsular Malaysia), High Court of Borneo (in East Malaysia), and a variety of lower courts. The Federal Court, consisting of six judges, is the highest court in the land. It has the authority to uphold the Constitution, review decisions referred by the Court of Appeals, and settle disputes between various states or between the federal government and a state. Federal judges are appointed by the king, who generally follows the recommendations of the prime minister. Malaysia's attorney general is known as the Principal Law Officer of the Crown, and is appointed by the king with the advice of the prime minister. The major duty of the attorney general is to advise the king and the cabinet on legal matters.

Although each of Malaysia's 13 states has elected assemblies, the powers of the state governments are curtailed by the federal constitution. However, the governments of Sabah and Sarawak retain some rights that the states of Peninsular Malaysia do not have, such as maintaining their own immigration controls.

Political Parties

Since Malaysia gained independence in 1957, the United Malays National Organization (UMNO) has dominated politics in Malaysia. Until 1973, UMNO was the largest member of the Alliance Party; that year, the Alliance Party was replaced with a broader coalition of parties, Barisan Nasional (National Front). UMNO remained the dominant party in the Barisan Nasional, which includes 13 other groups, such as Persatuan China Malaysia (Malayan Chinese Association, or MCA) and Kongresi

India Malaysia (Malayan Indian Congress, or MIC). The goal of the Barisan Nasional is to maintain a unified nation and uphold the traditions of the former Alliance party.

The current leader of the Barisan Nasional is Prime Minister Badawi, who also serves as head of UNMO. Most members of the coalition appreciate Badawi's moderation on issues concerning Islam. However, the moderate approach of Badawi and his predecessor Mahathir has resulted in the prime minister facing growing opposition from Parti Islam Semalaysia (Islamic Party of Malaysia, or PAS), which has taken an increasingly fundamentalist position over the past several decades. PAS is part of an opposition coalition of parties (Barisan Alternatif, or Alternative Front) that

Abdul Hadi Awang, leader of the Malaysian opposition party PAS, casts his vote during the March 2004 general election in Terengganu. Although his Islamic party has won some legislative successes, the Barisan Nasional coalition of parties, which is dominated by the United Malays National Organization, has maintained control over the federal government.

The flag of Malaysia (called *Jalur Gemilang*, or "Glorious Stripes") is composed of 14 red and white stripes. The crescent within the blue field is a traditional symbol of Islam, the national religion, while the 14-pointed star represents religious and political unity.

includes the Parti Keadilan Rakyat (People's Justice Party, or PKR) and Parti Tindakan Demokratik (Democratic Action Party, or DAP).

During the 1999 general elections, PAS—UMNO's major rival for the ethnic Malay vote—won 27 parliamentary seats and legislative control of the states of Terengganu and Kelantan. Following the election, moderate Muslim groups, women's groups, Christians, and other non-Muslim minorities watched in fear as the PAS attempted to impose Islamic law, known as *Sharia*, in Terengganu. (In 1993 the PAS had attempted to do the same thing in Kelantan, but the Malaysian government blocked the effort.) Under *Sharia*, the rights of women and non-Muslims are curtailed, and harsh punishments are proscribed for infractions of the law, such as amputation of the hands of those convicted of theft, stoning of those found guilty of adultery, and a death sentence for Muslims who convert to another religion. However, Mahathir and the Malaysian government again blocked the efforts of the PAS in Terengganu.

In the March 2004 general elections, Badawi and the UNMO party won an overwhelming victory. UNMO came away with 198 of the 219 parliamentary seats, while PAS retained just 7 parliamentary seats, lost legislative control of Terengganu, and barely retained control of Kelantan. The election results indicated that the vast majority of the Malaysian population intended to retain a moderate Islamic position.

Still, in the March 2008 parliamentary elections, opposition parties gained strength and support and greatly increased their representation in parliament. Apparently issues such as high inflation, rising crime rates, and ethnic tensions were detrimental to Badawi. The opposition coalition of DAP, PAS and PKR won 82 seats in Malaysia's parliament. As a result, Badawi's coalition lost its two-thirds majority—which is necessary to amend the Constitution—and control of five state assemblies. The opposition also took the four states of Penang, Kedah, Perak and Selangor, while retaining the opposition stronghold of Kelantan.

Nonetheless, with a simple majority of 140 seats in Parliament, Barisan Nasional were able to form the next government and Malaysia's Prime Minister Abdullah Ahmad Badawi was sworn in for a second term on March 10, 2008. After Najib Tun Razak won the presidency of UMNO in March 2009 party elections, Badawi stepped down as prime minister in favor of his deputy.

Religion in Malaysia

Religion is a fundamental aspect of Malaysian life, as the numerous mosques, temples, and churches throughout the country attest. Malaysia's religious beliefs and practices are strongly linked to ethnicity: most Chinese are Buddhists, most Indians are Hindu, and by law Malays must practice Islam. Because the government protects the religious freedoms of its minority groups, Malaysia is one of few Muslim nations where a variety of religions coexist in relative harmony. In contrast, Malaysia's

Malaysian Muslims participate in Friday prayers at a mosque.

neighbors—Indonesia, Thailand, and the Philippines—have been torn by religious strife in recent years due to the success of Muslim separatist movements.

However, Malaysia does not have total religious freedom. The government has imposed severe measures concerning the religious practices of its Muslim citizens. For example, Muslims must get official permission to marry people who do not practice Islam. Government leaders enact these measures to ensure that Muslims remain politically dominant as the country's majority group.

With about 1.25 billion followers, Islam is the second-largest religion in the world (after Christianity). The religion was founded in the Arabian Peninsula in the seventh century A.D. by a man named Muhammad, who taught that there is only one God, Allah. Muslims follow the teachings of Muhammad, whom they consider the last in a long line of prophets sent by God that also includes Moses and Jesus (the key figures in Judaism and Christianity, which like Islam are monotheistic religions.) God's messages to Muhammad are recorded in the Qur'an; Muslims also use stories from the lives of Muhammad and his companions as the basis for the way they are expected to live their own lives.

The core tenets of Islam are known as the Five Pillars. These include a declaration of faith that there is only one God and that Muhammad was His prophet; the performance of five ritual prayers at various times each day; the obligation of Muslims to give to the poor; self-sacrifice through fasting during the month of Ramadan (the ninth month of the Islamic lunar calendar); and the requirement that all Muslims must make a pilgrimage to the holy city of Mecca at least once during their lifetime, if they are physically and financially able to do so.

About 60 percent of Malaysians are Muslims, the overwhelming majority of whom are Malays. Most Malaysian Muslims follow a strict dress code, particularly during prayers and when entering a mosque. When

Muslim girls reach puberty they usually cover their hair with a long scarf called a *tudung*. In areas where Islamic practice is closely observed, such as in the northern states, some Muslim women wear the *purdah*, a black veil that completely covers the face as well as the head and upper body. Muslim men cover their heads with a brimless black hat called a *songkok* during worship and prayers. Men who have completed their pilgrimage to Mecca gain the privilege of wearing a special white skullcap.

Buddhists—most of whom are ethnic Chinese—are the second-largest religious group in Malaysia, making up about 19 percent of the population. Buddhism was founded during the late sixth century B.C. by Siddhartha Gautama (Buddha, "the Enlightened One") in northern India. From India, the religion spread to China and eventually, to Malaysia. Most Buddhist households in Malaysia feature small shrines where offerings of fruit, rice, and other delicacies are made to a variety of gods. Most Malaysian Buddhists follow Mahayana Buddhism, a form of Buddhism that is deeply infused with elements of Taoism, Confucianism, and **animism**. Mahayana, which literally means "Great Vehicle," is practiced by 56 percent of all Buddhists, making it the largest branch of Buddhism in the world. Ancestor worship is another element of traditional Chinese culture practiced by a small number of people in Malaysia.

Christianity was established in the first century A.D. Christians believe that Jesus Christ is the Son of God, who was sent to earth to die for the sins of mankind. Today, it is the largest religion in the world. The Portuguese brought Christianity to Malaysia when they captured Melaka in 1511. However, attempts to convert the Malays during the colonial era were rarely successful, particularly in Peninsular Malaysia, where Islam was the dominant faith. Today, about 9 percent of Malaysians, mostly living on Sabah and Sarawak, are Christians. Christianity is the main religion of East Malaysia, although many people there continue to practice their tribal religions as well.

Tribal religions in Malaysia are generally based on animism, an ancient belief system. Animists believe the world is filled with spirits—some good and some bad—which infuse and control everything in the physical world. A shaman or priestess usually serves as the medium to communicate with these spirits. Most animists in Malaysia live in rural areas and share a particularly close relationship with nature. The largest populations of animists are found in Sabah and Sarawak, where tribal traditions and rituals are vital elements of everyday life. Many religious rituals and festivals are linked to the harvest of rice, which is held sacred by East Malaysians. Animists also place great significance on ancestor worship; they believe their ancestors can intercede on their behalf in the realm of spirits.

About 6 percent of Malaysians—mostly ethnic Indians—are Hindus. The Hindu faith is governed by a caste system that determines a person's social status. This status is inherited at birth and cannot be changed. The religion's rigid class structure generally appeals more to the upper classes, and thus most of the earliest Hindu converts in Malaysia were Malay royalty, with Islam having greater appeal among the common folk. However, during the 1800s the British brought numerous Indian workers to Malaysia to work in the rubber plantations. Because most of the Indian laborers were members of the lower social classes, they intentionally did not strictly observe the caste system. As a result, there is no distinctive caste system among most Hindu communities in Malaysia today.

The Economy

In less than five decades since gaining its independence, Malaysia has undergone dramatic and progressive economic change. During the early years, the nation's economy was primarily based upon agriculture and mining. However, using the wealth of its rich natural resources, Malaysia has been able to shift its economic focus to the more profitable manufacturing and industry sectors. In 1970, agriculture and mining accounted for 42.7 percent of the **gross domestic product (GDP)** while manufacturing accounted for 13 percent of the GDP. By 1999 agriculture and mining had dropped to 7.3 percent of the GDP while manufacturing rose to 30 percent. As Malaysia continued to diversify its economy, employment rates rose and poverty levels dropped. Between 1991 and 1997, Malaysia's poverty level fell from 16.5 percent to 6.1 percent.

The economy has suffered occasional setbacks, however. Like many of its neighbors, Malaysia was hit hard by the Asian financial crisis during the late 1990s. Between mid-1997 and early 1998, the ringgit (Malaysia's official currency) depreciated by 56 percent and the stock market plunged by 50 percent. By the end of 1998, the country's GDP had shrunk by more than 8 percent. The nation gradually recovered, and by 2004, the GDP was again experiencing robust growth.

Today, private enterprise, which is supported by the government through a variety of programs, is the backbone of the national economy. The Malaysian government also encourages international trade and foreign investment. Currently, the United States is Malaysia's largest trading partner and largest foreign investor.

Natural Resources

Malaysia is blessed with a variety of natural resources such as timber, minerals, natural gas, and oil. Global demand for timber and construction materials tripled during the 1990s. In 2001, Malaysia emerged as the world's third-largest exporter of logs after Russia and the United States. In order to keep up with global demand and increase its export earnings, Malaysia's timber industry has progressed from exporting unfinished timber to more profitable endeavors such as manufacturing furniture, veneers, plywood, and a variety of construction materials.

Malaysia's mineral wealth includes tin, gold, copper, bauxite, iron ore, and coal, most of which are found in Peninsular Malaysia. Historically, tin has been the most important resource in the mineral sector and remained a major source of foreign income during the 19th and 20th centuries. In 1979, Malaysia produced 31 percent of the world's tin supply and the mining industry employed more than 41,000 people. However, the depletion of tin

For most of the 20th century Malaysia's economy was dependent on the export of raw materials. In this 1957 photo, Malaysian managers at the Dato Kramat Works in Penang examine tin ingots waiting to be shipped.

The Economy of Malaysia

Gross Domestic Product (GDP*): $386.6 billion
GDP per capita: $15,300
Inflation: 5.8%
Natural resources: tin, petroleum, timber, copper, iron ore, natural gas, bauxite
Industry (44.6% of GDP): Peninsular Malaysia—rubber and oil palm processing and manufacturing, light manufacturing industry, electronics, tin mining and smelting, logging and processing timber; Sabah—logging, petroleum production; Sarawak—agriculture processing, petroleum production and refining, logging
Agriculture (9.7% of GDP): Peninsular Malaysia—rubber, palm oil, cocoa, rice; Sabah—subsistence crops, rubber, timber, coconuts, rice; Sarawak—rubber, pepper; timber
Services (45.7% of GDP): civil service, public services, utilities, transportation, communications, education and health services, engineering, consulting, architecture, construction, insurance, finance, tourism, hotels, restaurants
Foreign trade:
    Imports—$156.2 billion: electronic equipment, petroleum and liquefied natural gas, wood and wood products, palm oil, rubber, textiles, chemicals
    Exports—$195.7 billion: electronics, machinery, petroleum products, plastics, vehicles, iron and steel products, chemicals
Currency exchange rate: U.S. $1 = 3.58 Malaysian riggits (2009)

*GDP, or gross domestic product, is the total value of goods and services produced in a country annually.

All figures are 2008 estimates unless otherwise noted.

Source: CIA World Factbook, 2009.

deposits combined with low global market prices and high operating costs contributed to the decline of this once-vital industry. By 1994, Malaysia's tin production had fallen by 90 percent and only about 3,000 people were employed in the industry. Today, Malaysia doesn't export much tin, but instead uses it for domestic industries such as tin-plating and electronics.

Vast reserves of oil and natural gas were discovered off the coasts of Sabah, Sarawak, and Terengganu in the early 1970s. By 2001, Malaysia had the 12th-largest natural gas reserves and the 27th-largest crude oil reserves in the world. Today, according to the country's Energy Information Administration, Malaysia's natural gas reserves total about 75 trillion cubic feet and its crude oil reserves total 3 billion barrels. Currently, the country is pursuing ambitious plans to expand the oil industry by opening ultra-deepwater offshore areas for international oil companies to explore. (Ultra-deepwater areas are deeper than 3,281 feet, or 1,000 meters.)

Agriculture

Currently, agriculture employs about 13 percent of Malaysia's workforce and accounts for 9.7 percent of the GDP. There are two main types of farms in Malaysia—small holdings, usually consisting of less than five acres (two hectares), and commercial plantations, most of which are owned by large companies. Because much of Malaysia is covered by rainforests and mountains, only about 6 percent of the land is considered arable, or suitable for agriculture. Due to the lack of arable land and the high cost of fertilizers, it is cheaper for Malaysia to import some of its food products from neighboring countries rather than growing its own. In addition, the shortage of grazing land necessitates the import of livestock products such as beef. However, in the past decade Malaysia has shown its desire to become self-sufficient in food products through a variety of creative measures, such as agroforestry and growing new kinds of crops.

Agroforestry, a practice that the government heavily promotes, involves planting crops and raising livestock in or around forests. It has many benefits, such as increasing the productivity of each piece of land while at the same time preserving natural resources. Malaysian farmers are now raising short-term crops such as pineapples, chili, corn, and mushrooms alongside rubber trees, oil palms, bamboo, rattan (thorny, climbing palms), medicinal trees, and valuable hardwoods such as teak. Most of Malaysia's beef cattle are owned by small farmers who don't have enough land for grazing pastures. Instead, they use creative methods to feed their livestock such as allowing their cattle to forage beneath tree crops. The government encourages this practice, which reduces the use of herbicides and lowers weeding costs by 20 to 40 percent. Oil palm plantations have proven particularly useful for feeding cattle because the plants that spring up beneath the trees are rich in nutrients, particularly protein.

Malaysia's tropical climate and plentiful rainfall creates the ideal environment for growing the nation's two most important cash crops—rubber and palm oil. Traditionally, Malaysia exported natural rubber and palm oil as raw commodities. Today, the processing of these commodities into a variety of useful products for both global and domestic markets is an important industry that is undergoing dynamic growth. During 2004, Malaysia's rubber production rose by 21.9 percent while global market prices surged, resulting in greater revenues. In 2007, rubber products accounted for 1.7 percent of Malaysia's total exports and 2.3 percent of the country's exports from the manufacturing sector.

The continued success of the rubber industry can be attributed in part to the Malaysian Rubber Board (MRB), the world's largest single-commodity research organization. Its current research projects include finding innovative

Many multinational corporations have opened factories in Malaysia. Here, a woman prepares color television sets on a production line at the Sony factory in Kajang.

ways to use rubber, which shows vast potential in the medical, pharmaceuticals, and cosmetics industries. The MRB also promotes natural rubber for industrial applications such as bridge bearings and seismic construction bearings, which are used in earthquake-prone areas.

Manufacturing and Industry

During the 1960s, Malaysia started producing goods that it once imported, marking the industrialization of its economy. These items included food products, beverages, tobacco, building materials, chemicals, and plastics. By producing these goods the country could save on

> In 1985, Malaysia proudly unveiled the Proton Saga, its national car. The government presented the sedan as a symbol of Malaysia's resolve to transform itself into a fully industrialized country.

import expenditures and use the available funds to further expand its industrial base. An additional benefit was the creation of many new jobs and a gradual decline in unemployment.

During the 1980s, Malaysia's economic policies focused on diversifying its industrial base and adding heavy industries such as steel, concrete, and motor vehicles. Today, industry employs about 36 percent of the workforce (over a million people) and accounts for 44.6 percent of the nation's GDP.

Another vital and fast-growing industry is information technology (IT), which relies heavily on exports to the global market. In 2001, the international IT market suffered a steep downturn, taking Malaysia's export-dependent economy with it. By this time, Malaysia had developed its IT sector to an astonishing size, becoming one of the world's largest producers of electronic and electrical products. When Malaysia's exports declined by about 11 percent in 2001, the GDP grew by a mere 0.5 percent during the same year. However, the global economy rebounded during the following year and Malaysia's economy also bounced back. In April 2004, electrical and electronic products were the largest foreign exchange earners in the country, accounting for 49.4 percent (19.6 billion ringgits) of total exports. Malaysia's major trading partners in the IT sector include the United States, Singapore, Japan, Hong Kong, China, and Thailand. Currently, the nation has ambitious plans to transform its IT sector from a labor-intensive assembly operation to a research- and development-based industry.

Services

The services sector employs about 51 percent of Malaysia's workforce and contributes 45.7 percent of the GDP. This sector includes the civil service, utilities, transportation, communications and media, publishing, hotels and restaurants, health services, and tourism.

Because Malaysia is blessed with spectacular scenery, tourism shows promise of becoming a major contributor to the economy. In recent years, however, global events such as the 2001 terrorist attacks in the United States, the 2002 attacks in Bali, and the appearance of Severe Acute Respiratory Syndrome (SARS) in 2003 have contributed to a worldwide decline in tourism. Despite these problems, the Malaysian Tourism Board reported that more than 5 million foreign visitors came to the country in 2004, an increase of more than 50 percent. Numerous visitors from Singapore (who make up a large majority of Malaysia's tourists) pour over the causeway to Johor during weekends and holiday. Domestic tourism is also on the rise.

Overall, Malaysia's economy grew by more than 5 percent in 2008 despite long-term economic slowdowns in Japan and a sharp downward inflection in the United States, both of which are key trading partners as well as crucial sources of foreign investment. Malaysia has recently attained newly industrialized country (NIC) status, which means it has a high-growth, industrial economy. Today, Malaysia is a middle-income country with a relatively high standard of living. By promoting a diverse industry-driven economy, encouraging international trade and foreign investments, as well as developing the country's natural resources, the government hopes to sustain Malaysia's economic growth while allowing its people to share equally in the nation's prosperity.

KASTHURI PAL

PEMBUAT KAIN PELIKAT SA
உரிகாட்டகள் தூரி பளயகாட
NO : 3. JALAN MELAYU 5010
TALIPON NO : 2929740

A man stands in the doorway of a shop in Kuala Lumpur's Indian Quarter. Because of its history as a trading center, Malaysia has great ethnic and religious diversity. Despite the differences between these groups, Malaysians have managed to forge a peaceful and prosperous society.

5 The People

In 2004, Malaysia's population numbered over 23.5 million people, with 85 percent living in Peninsular Malaysia. Malaysia's diverse population can be divided into four major groups: Malay, Chinese, Indian, and native tribal peoples.

The Malays, or *bumiputeras*, are the largest ethnic group in the country, accounting for 58 percent of the total population. The Chinese make up 24 percent of the population and the Indians account for about 8 percent. Despite the historical trading ties, it was not until the 19th century that members of these groups settled in significant numbers. The Indian population of Malaysia is primarily descended from the Hindu Tamils of southern India and lives mainly in urban communities along the western coast of the peninsula.

Indigenous tribal peoples make up about 5 percent of the nation's population. Most of Malaysia's indigenous peoples prefer to be identified by their specific tribes, but they are usually classified into several large groups. The major tribal groups of Malaysia are the Orang Asli and Semang peoples of Peninsular Malaysia and the Dayak peoples of Sabah and Sarawak. Tribal peoples represent the majority of the population in both Sabah and Sarawak, and it is estimated that there are over 200 different tribes on the island of Borneo. The major Dayak tribes of Malaysia include the Iban (Sea Dayaks) and Bidayuh (Land Dayaks) of Sarawak and the Kadazan Dusun of Sabah.

Language and Education

Malaysia's national language is Bahasa Melayu, or Malay, which is used in all official government business. (Malay is also the official language of neighboring Brunei, as well as one of the four official languages of Singapore.) In addition to Malay, a number of languages reflecting the nation's diverse ethnic composition are spoken in Malaysia. The Chinese primarily speak the Hokkein, Hakka, and Cantonese dialects, while the Indian communities mainly converse in Tamil, Malayalam, and Hindi. The indigenous peoples of East Malaysia speak a variety of tribal languages, including numerous regional dialects. English is also widely spoken in Malaysia and is often used when different ethnic communities converse with one another. Most school classes on the postsecondary level are also taught in English.

Malaysians place great emphasis on education. The nation boasts a literacy rate of about 89 percent, one of the highest rates among the world's Muslim nations. The government provides 11 years of free public schooling. School attendance is not required by law in Malaysia, but over 99 percent of all six-year-olds are enrolled in primary school and more than 92 percent of students continue on to secondary school.

Malaysia's innovative educational system uses a flexible and career-oriented approach. Primary schools teach basic skills such as reading,

Indian, Malay, and Chinese students study a workbook together at a school in Kuala Lumpur. The government of Malaysia places a strong emphasis on public education, and as a result Malaysians are among the best-educated people in the Muslim world.

writing, mathematics, and basic sciences, but secondary schools focus on career preparation. Starting in primary school, students are regularly assessed through examinations that highlight both their strengths and weaknesses. A number of vocational and technical schools are available

The People of Malaysia

Population: 25,715,819
Ethnic groups: Malay 50.4%, Chinese 23.7%, indigenous 11%, Indian 7.1%, others 7.8% (2004 est.)
Religions: Muslim 60.4%, Buddhist 19.2%, Christian 9.1%, Hindu 6.3%, Confucianism, Taoism, other traditional Chinese religions 2.6%, other or unknown 1.5%, none 0.8% (2000 census)
Age structure:
    0–14 years: 31.4%
    15–64 years: 63.6%
    65 years and over: 5%
Population growth rate: 1.72%
Birth rate: 22.44 births/1,000 population
Infant mortality rate: 15.87 deaths/1,000 live births
Death rate: 5.02 deaths/1,000 population
Life expectancy at birth:
    total population: 73.29 years
    male: 70.56 years
    female: 76.21 years
Total fertility rate: 2.95 children born/woman
Literacy: 88.7% (2000 census)

All figures are 2009 estimates unless otherwise indicated.
Source: Adapted from CIA World Factbook, 2009.

to secondary school graduates, many of which focus on information technology.

Malaysia's first university, the University of Malaya, was founded in Singapore in 1949. Today, there are dozens of national and private universities and colleges throughout the country. In addition, there are a variety of international schools, including British, American, Japanese, German, Taiwanese, Indonesian, and Saudi Arabian institutions, which cater to the families of international investors, businessmen, and professionals.

Lifestyle

Malaysian families are closely knit and usually have strong ties to their communities. Traditional Malay culture centers on the *kampung,* or village. Because fishing is a major economic activity, most villages are located near the mouth of a river. Traditional Malay homes are built of wood and are usually perched high on stilts to protect them from flooding. The Dayaks of East Malaysia typically live in longhouses, a name that aptly describes the long rambling structures that can accommodate 20 to 50 families. The longhouse has a veranda running the length of the building that serves as a communal gathering place. Today, some modern longhouses feature glass windows, electricity, and indoor plumbing.

Many rural communities have only a single television, and watching TV is often a community event. Village and longhouse communities have either village or house elders who settle disputes, oversee sanitation projects, and uphold the cultural traditions of the people. Most Chinese Malaysian villages appoint a Kapitan Cina (Captain of the Chinese) for the same duties.

Urban homes in Malaysia range from pricey condominiums with all the modern comforts to ramshackle squatter settlements on the outskirts of cities, where newly arrived migrants live temporarily until they can find work.

Malaysia's tropical climate makes it possible to find fresh foods all year round. The national fare utilizes the bountiful gifts of nature in a variety of innovative ways. Malaysian food is usually spicy in flavor and can be divided into Malay, Chinese, and Indian cuisine. However, some dishes are a tasty blend of cultural influences such as Indian-Muslim and Malay-Chinese. Rice is the staple food of the Malaysian diet and is eaten at least once a day. A favorite Malaysian dish is *nasi lemak,* rice cooked with coconut milk and fragrant herbs like ginger or lemon grass. *Nasi lemak* is eaten any time of day and is widely sold in restaurants and food stalls throughout the country. The creamy dish, often wrapped neatly in a banana leaf, is served with spicy condiments and a variety of meats including chicken, beef, or cuttlefish.

Malay Muslims obey Islamic prohibitions on drinking alcohol and eating pork, and Hindus and most Buddhists do not eat beef. However, virtually everyone eats fish, which is the primary source of protein in the Malaysian diet. Malaysians enjoy fishing for both economic purposes and leisure. Those living in rural areas use fishing lines, traps woven of rattan or bamboo, and nets stretched across a small river mouth to catch a meal of fresh fish.

Because Malaysia's climate is tropical all year round, Malaysian clothing is lightweight, loose, and comfortable. Today, many people wear Western-style suits and dresses, especially for work in the cities. Traditional Malay women's clothing includes the *baju kurung,* a flowing knee-length tunic that is worn over a long skirt. Malay men wear the *baju melayu,* a loose airy shirt worn over a pair of lightweight trousers. For special occasions such as prayer and religious festivals they add a colorful brocade belt tied around the waist. Malaysian children wear uniforms to school and it is considered immodest for children who have reached puberty to wear short pants that expose their thighs. Indian women are often seen in a brightly hued, gossamer *sari,* while many Chinese women favor the *samfoo,* a comfortable yet form-fitting suit consisting of a tailored blouse and matching trousers.

Arts and Leisure

The arts of Malaysia are a dynamic blend of cultural influences. Storytelling is an ancient art that has helped preserve the country's history

These Malaysian children are wearing traditional headgear. The boy wears a black cap called a *songok*, while the girl wears a traditional scarf, called a *tudung*, which covers her hair and neck.

and traditions. In the days before reading, writing, radio, and television, storytellers were among the most popular entertainers in the country. Today, community elders continue the storytelling tradition, and epic tales of heroism and sacrifice are still popular features of many festivals.

Malaysians listen to a variety of music ranging from traditional folk music to Western classical to modern pop. Traditional Malay music was greatly influenced by Chinese and Islamic forms, and reached its heyday during the Melaka Sultanate when music was a vital part of ritualistic court ceremonies as well as everyday village life. Even today, the royal courts of

Peninsular Malaysia maintain their own music and dance troupes, and music is an integral part of the nation's festivals, drama, and dance. *Gamelan* is a form of traditional music that is played during ceremonial occasions. It incorporates xylophones, gongs, and a variety of drums. The *gendang*, or drum, is the backbone of traditional music and the only featured instrument in some forms of Malay music. One of the most widely used drums in Malaysia is the *kompang*, a goatskin-covered hand drum that resembles a tambourine. Other traditional instruments are the *sape*, which resembles a lute and is popular in East Malaysia, and the *rebab*, a type of three-stringed violin that is typically played during dance-dramas.

Many of Malaysia's dances show the influences of Thai, Indian, and Portuguese cultures. The *joget*, Malaysia's most popular traditional dance, stems from Portuguese folk dancing and features lively music and fast, stylized movements. Traditionally, it was only performed by men, but today the animated dance is usually performed by couples and is popular at weddings, festivals, and other celebrations. *Mak yong*, a combination of music, dance, and drama, is the traditional dance-drama of Malaysia. It originated in the state of Kelantan as a classic form of court entertainment, and is usually performed by female dancers who play both male and female roles. This custom dates back to ancient times when only women were allowed in the sultan's harem.

Silat is the Malay art of self-defense but it is also an exciting dance form that combines deadly sparring moves with graceful choreography and music. The dance is a twisting, leaping display of grace, strength, and flexibility. The *tarian lilin* (candle dance) is a particularly beautiful performance that features dancing women holding a lit candle in each hand. The dance, which originated in Indonesia, tells the story of a beautiful maiden who lost her engagement ring. The stylized movements of the dance, which include swaying, bending, and kneeling, represent her search for the ring by the light of a candle.

One of the most ancient forms of traditional theater in Malaysia is *wayang kulit* (shadow puppetry). It is also popular in Indonesia, Thailand, Cambodia, India, and Turkey. A major theater event, *wayang kulit* is performed using large puppets made of stiff leather (usually goatskin, cow, or buffalo hide). The puppets are manipulated with sticks behind a white curtain that is illuminated with lanterns. The puppet shadows are brought to life by the manipulations and voice of the puppeteer, who is called the *tok dalang*. The play is accompanied by Malay music that heightens the tension and adds to the drama.

Making and flying kites were once popular post-harvest pastimes of rice farmers that have become international events. Today, the kite festival in Kelantan draws visitors from all over the world, and the state boasts

Top spinning is a popular Malaysian pastime. It takes a great deal of skill to throw a top so that it lands on the square clay platform. The best throwers are called *tukang gasing* ("masters of the top").

some of the finest kite makers in the nation. Over the years, kite making has become more intricate as craftspeople continue to display their skills with increasingly complicated patterns and shapes. However, the traditional crescent moon-shaped *wau bulan* (moon kite) of Kelantan remains the most popular design in Malaysia.

Top spinning, called *gasing* in Malaysia, is another national pastime that started as a post-harvest leisure activity. Traditionally, spinning competitions were held between neighboring villages; now they are held on a national level. Top spinning takes dexterity, timing, and strength because the tops can weigh up to 11 pounds (5 kg). The tops are wound with a cord and tossed onto a surface to start them spinning. Skillful spinners can keep their tops whirling for up to an hour and a half!

Another game of skill and physical dexterity is *sepak takraw*, one of the most popular sports in Malaysia. Similar to the American game of hacky sack with elements of volleyball and soccer, *sepak takraw* involves players using their feet, thighs, shoulders, heads—everything but their hands—to hit a small rattan ball back and forth across a net. Badminton and soccer are also among the most popular sports in the nation. Malaysia boasts one of the finest national badminton teams in the world and has won the coveted Thomas Cup five times.

Malaysians are adept at a variety of handicrafts, such as batik weaving, wood carving, pottery, and metalwork. These skills have given rise to a number of flourishing cottage industries. Batik is a form of textile design that is made by applying wax to fabric. While the rest of fabric is dyed, the wax designs remain uncolored. Rich, vibrant colors and fanciful swirling designs inspired by nature are the hallmarks of this ancient craft that originated in Indonesia. Batik is the official textile design of Malaysia and its popularity now extends throughout the world. Kelantan and Terengganu are particularly famous for their elegant batik, which is hailed as the finest in the world.

Competitors jump to kick the ball over the net during a *sepak takraw* match at sunset.

Another specialty of Kelantan and Terengganu is *kain songket* (cloth of gold), a traditional handwoven fabric that sparkles with gold and silver threads. Malaysian women also practice *mengkuang* weaving, which involves making a variety of useful household objects from readily avail-

> One of the most important Malay cultural symbols is the *keris*, a double-edged dagger with an elaborately carved hilt and wavy blade. Once a widely used weapon, the *keris* is now a status symbol of Malay royalty as well as a national icon that features prominently in many legends.

able materials such as bamboo, rattan, and tropical leaves. One of the most famous crafts of East Malaysia is *pua kumbu,* the traditional fabric of the Iban people. The dye is made from natural materials such roots, bark, berries, and leaves. Dye formulas are closely guarded family secrets that are passed down from mother to daughter.

Wood carving is one of the oldest traditional art forms in the country and Malaysian wood-carvers are among the finest in the world. Combining form and function, finely wrought carvings adorn the doors, walls, and windows of traditional Malay homes as well as public buildings. Malaysians are also highly accomplished in the art of metalsmithing and create numerous works of art in gold, silver, brass, and pewter with a distinctive regional style. Pewter is made primarily of tin and the art of tinsmithing is a traditional craft that is still practiced today.

Popular Celebrations and Festivals

Malaysians celebrate a variety of holidays and festivals throughout the year. Many are linked to religious rituals while others celebrate historic events, popular activities, or seasonal events such as the annual harvest. Malaysia has an open-door policy for religious festivals and all other celebrations. People of all faiths and ethnic origins, including foreign visitors, are welcome to celebrate together. The Malaysian Tourist Board will even

arrange a host family for international visitors who plan to attend a major event.

The dates for some of Malaysia's festivals and holidays vary from year to year because they are set according to ethnic custom. The Chinese and Muslims, for example, use lunar calendars. Some of Malaysia's public holidays are national while others are observed only in certain states. National holidays include National Day, which is celebrated on August 31 with parades, speeches, and festivities to commemorate Malaysia's independence, and Labor Day, which is celebrated each year in May. Pesta Malaysia (Malaysia Fest) is a two-week event celebrating the nation's culture. Even many non-Christian Malaysians celebrate Christmas, the birth of Jesus, each year on December 25 with Christmas trees, gifts, and church services. The birthdays of the prophet Muhammad and the king of Malaysia are also public holidays.

Observed throughout Malaysia, Hari Raya Puasa is a monthlong festival that celebrates the end of Ramadan, the Muslim month of fasting. *Hari Raya* means "day of celebration" and although it lasts for an entire month, only the first two days are designated as a public holiday. Muslims begin the first day of Hari Raya by donning their finest new clothes and gathering in the local mosques for prayers. Next, they usually visit the cemeteries to pray for deceased loved ones and tend the graves. The rest of the day is spent visiting friends and family or receiving guests. The highlight of the festival is a celebration feast of specially prepared foods. Some Muslim families hold open house throughout the month, inviting friends and neighbors from other religious backgrounds to share in the joyous occasion.

Another important Muslim holiday is Hari Raya Haji (Festival of the Pilgrimage). Held each year during the 12th month of the Muslim calendar, the public holiday commemorates the patriarch Abraham's willingness to sacrifice his son to God. The festival is particularly special

A Malaysian woman examines a display of *nasi lemak* and other popular traditional foods sold at a Ramadan bazaar in Kuala Lumpur. During this month, Muslims do not eat from dawn to dusk, then break their fasts with specially prepared dishes.

for those who have made the pilgrimage to Mecca (*hajj*) and marks the end of the pilgrimage period.

Chinese New Year is celebrated in January or February, depending on the date set by the Chinese lunar calendar. Preparations for the grand event begin months in advance as homes are cleaned from top to bottom and decorated with red paper lanterns, colorful banners painted with lucky calligraphy symbols, fresh flowers, and kumquat trees. On New Year's Eve, family members gather from all over the country to share a lively reunion feast. Symbolic gifts are exchanged, including mandarin oranges, the traditional Chinese symbol for gold or wealth. Children happily receive red envelopes of "lucky money" called *angpow*. Because firecrackers and fireworks have been banned in Malaysia, many towns use recorded sounds of exploding firecrackers to ring in the New Year. The Chingay parade on New Year's Day is the highlight of the festival. The lively beat of drums, cymbals, and gongs accompany stilt walkers, acrobats, and colorful floats as they parade through the streets. The parade also features the dragon dance and lion dance, crowd favorites that represent two of the most powerful forces of Chinese mythology.

Another important Chinese celebration is the Mooncake Festival, which commemorates the overthrow of the Mongol Dynasty in China during the 14th century. The festival is usually held during August or September. On the night of the festival, children carry brightly lit lanterns of all colors and shapes in a lively procession through the streets. Mooncakes—rich, round pastries filled with sweet bean paste, lotus nut paste, or salted egg yolk—are exchanged and eaten throughout the month of the festival.

Deepavali (Festival of Lights) is a Hindu festival celebrating the triumph of good over evil. It is observed each year during the seventh month of the Hindu calendar (usually October or November). During Deepavali, Malaysian homes and gardens twinkle with dozens of sparkling lights. Some people use traditional oil lamps made of clay called *vikku*, while others use colorful electric bulbs or candles. Richly hued Hindu symbols called *kolam* adorn the walls and entryways of homes, businesses, and temples. Some *kolam* are painted or drawn while

A Malaysian Hindu penitent sits in a trance while his skin is pierced with pins during a Thaipusam celebration outside the Batu Caves.

others are made with colored grains of rice. On Deepavali, Hindu families rise before sunrise and cleanse themselves with a ritual oil bath. After a visit to the local temple, friends and family gather from all over Malaysia for a celebration feast.

Thaipusam is another Hindu festival celebrated in Malaysia. The festival is held in January or February when the constellation of Pusam, the Hindu star of well-being, rises in the eastern sky. The biggest celebration is held at the Batu Caves on the outskirts of Kuala Lumpur; in 2000, nearly a million people came to the caves from all over the world for this festival. During Thaipusam, which was introduced by the Indian Tamils during the late 1800s, Hindu devotees carry the *kavadi* (a wood or metal frame adorned with colored paper, tinsel, fresh flowers, and fruits) up 271 grueling steps to the Batu Caves Temple. The *kavadi* is balanced on metal skewers inserted into the backs and arms of the carriers or held in place with metal hooks and chains (also inserted through the skin). Devotees also typically skewer their own cheeks, tongues, and foreheads as penance and a demonstration of their faith.

The Gawai Dayak Festival is held each year in Sarawak by the Dayak peoples during May or early June to mark the end of the rice growing season. The celebration is a merry affair with plenty of rice wine, music, and dance. The Ngajat Lesong is a special dance performed by men who display their strength and skill by lifting a heavy rice mortar (a tool for pounding rice) with their teeth.

Vesak Day is celebrated on May 25 by Malaysian Buddhists and commemorates the birth, enlightenment, and death of the Buddha.

High-rise office buildings, such as the ones in the background of this photo, dominate the skyline of Kuala Lumpur. The capital of Malaysia, Kuala Lumpur is also the largest city in the federation, with a population of about 1.8 million people.

6

Cities and Communities

$\mathcal{M}$ alaysia's major cities grew and prospered as a result of trade. Some cities were blessed with natural harbors or located near trade routes. Others were endowed with natural resources such as tin ore—a major trading commodity since ancient times—or fertile soils suitable for agriculture.

Like many developing nations, Malaysia experienced a high migration to urban areas after it began industrializing its economy in the 1960s. People from rural areas, as well as from neighboring countries, began pouring into the cities to find employment. Today, about 59 percent of the nation's population is urban, compared to 25 percent in 1970. Low urban unemployment rates and the nation's dynamic industrial growth continue to spur the expansion of Malaysia's most prosperous communities.

Kuala Lumpur

The city of Kuala Lumpur is Malaysia's official capital city. With a population of more than 1.8 million people in 2008, it is by far the largest city in the nation. It is located in the Wilayah Persekutuan federal district within the state of Selangor, about midway down the western flank of the peninsula.

Kuala Lumpur means "muddy **confluence**" in Malay, and the original city was located high atop a riverbank at the confluence of the Klang and Gombak Rivers. The rivers had left rich deposits of tin ore along their shores, a discovery that was made by a group of Chinese prospectors in 1857. The richest mines were located in what is now the city of Ampang. Kuala Lumpur, located a little over a mile (2 km) to the west, was first settled as a trading depot to supply the miners and their families with necessities in exchange for tin.

Tin was a valuable commodity because of the industrial revolution in Europe and the United States, so Kuala Lumpur quickly developed into a bustling shantytown. However, like many early mining towns, Kuala Lumpur was a disorderly and dangerous place as several Chinese families competed for dominance over the tin trade. Yap Ah Loy, who became Kuala Lumpur's third Kapitan Cina in 1868, oversaw the city's transformation from an unruly shantytown into the largest and most prosperous city in Selangor.

However, this transformation would take decades because of various catastrophies. In 1857 the sultan of Selangor had died without naming an heir, and during the 1860s Malay rulers argued over tin revenues and the leadership of the region. The Selangor Civil War began in 1867 and lasted for six years. The fighting was centered in the Kuala Lumpur region, and much of the settlement was destroyed. The British, who administered most of the Malay Peninsula, ultimately intervened, establishing a peace treaty known as the Pangkor Agreement in 1874. The treaty officially ended the war and appointed Sir Frank Swettenham as Resident of Selangor. The leader holding this office was responsible for overseeing all matters "other than those touching Malay religion and custom."

While Swettenham worked to make Kuala Lumpur an administrative center, Yap Ah Loy took charge of redevelopment after the war. He convinced the Chinese to stay and rebuild the city, imported thousands of laborers from China and neighboring Malay states, and encouraged the farmers to grow rice to feed the growing workforce.

In 1880, the British named Kuala Lumpur the capital of Selangor, but the following year a devastating fire swept through the city, burning it to the ground. Once again, Yap Ah Loy rebuilt the city and constructed the first school and a shelter for those left homeless by the fire. Because of his success quelling local rebellions, building hospitals and homes, and maintaining the peace in the mining region, Yap Ah Loy is often hailed as the founding father of Kuala Lumpur.

After Yap Ah Loy's death in 1885, Swettenham continued his legacy of development and the city prospered. When Britain formed the Federated Malay States in 1896, Kuala Lumpur was named the capital. In less than four decades, Kuala Lumpur had grown from a shantytown into the administrative and commercial hub of the nation.

When Malaysia gained its independence from Britain in 1957, a large crowd gathered at Kuala Lumpur's Dataran Merdeka (Independence Square) to watch as the Union Jack was lowered and Malaysia's new flag was hoisted in its place. The next two decades saw explosive growth as the population of the city more than doubled, swelling from 451,728 people in 1970 to over a million people in 1991. In 1974, Kuala Lumpur was

designated as part of a federal territory of Malaysia, which means it is administered separately from the rest of Selangor.

The executive branch of the government was moved to Putrajaya, Malaysia's new administrative capital, in 1999. However, the legislative branch and the judiciary are still seated in Kuala Lumpur, which remains the federal capital.

Kuala Lumpur is often called the "gateway to Malaysia," because it is the transportation hub as well as the commercial center of the nation. A railway links the city with Thailand to the north and Singapore to the south, and the Kuala Lumpur International Airport (KLIA) is an architectural masterpiece that covers an area of 38 square miles (100 sq km), making it one of the largest airports in the world.

The city is a fascinating mix of culture and technology. Within a vast area of 94 square miles (244 sq km) is a variety of colonial buildings and national monuments as well as ethnic markets and modern shopping malls. Towering majestically over the city skyline, the 1,483-foot (452-meter) Petronas Twin Towers is the pride of the nation. Officially opened in August 1999, the building's design was inspired by traditional Islamic geometric forms. The exterior of the 88-story building is constructed of horizontal ribbons of steel and glass that shimmer in the sun. For a few years, Petronas Towers was the tallest building in the world. (It was surpassed in 2003 by the Taipei 101 Tower in Taiwan.)

Other national landmarks include the Sultan Abdul Samad Building, which was constructed in the late 1800s to house the British administration. Today the Moorish-style building with its majestic clock tower and shiny copper dome houses the Malaysian Supreme Court and the Textile Museum. Standing on a hill overlooking the Klang River is the Istana Negara, the official residence of the king of Malaysia. The National Mosque was opened in 1965 and features a distinct central roof that resembles a partially opened umbrella. The 18 points around the roof edge symbolize each of the nation's 13 states and the five pillars of Islam.

The Multimedia Super Corridor

The Multimedia Super Corridor (MSC) is a government-designated zone devoted to the development of information technology. The corridor, which covers 290 square miles (750 sq km) and is roughly the size of Singapore, stretches from Kuala Lumpur City Centre southward to the city's international airport. The driving force behind the MSC vision was

Tourists pose for a group photo in front of the landmark Sultan Abdul Samad building at Independence Square in Kuala Lumpur. In recent years tourism has been a growing sector of Malaysia's economy.

Mahathir bin Mohamad. The MSC was founded on an ambitious plan to transform the region's plantation-based economy into a world-class provider of information technology. The ultimate goal of the MSC is to propel Malaysia toward fully industrialized nation status by the year 2020. To achieve this goal the Malaysian government offers attractive tax breaks to foreign investors, high-speed computer links to the major cities, and high-speed rail transport throughout the MSC. Today, more than 60 world-class international companies, including IBM, Microsoft, and Lucent Technologies, operate facilities in the MSC.

Two cities located within the corridor, Putrajaya and Cyberjaya, are "smart cities"—cities that use microcomputers and other electronic intelligence to facilitate the operation of transportation, communication, and administrative infrastructures. The Malaysian government decided to move its operations to Putrajaya to ease the growing congestion in Kuala Lumpur as well as to facilitate the growth of the MSC.

Putrajaya was home to more than 50,000 residents by 2007; however, the city is still undergoing development and is not expected to be completed until 2010, when the total population is predicted to exceed 300,000 people. The city was designed to preserve and highlight its natural surroundings, and about 40 percent of the area is covered with lush greenery. A number of botanical gardens, lakes, and parks were designed to provide relaxing retreats from the bustle of modern life. In the center of the city lies the Putrajaya Wetlands, which is dominated by Putrajaya Lake. This man-made lake serves as a natural cooling system for the city as well as a recreational area for fishing and water sports.

Dataran Putra (Putra Square) is the centerpiece of Putrajaya and one of the most beautiful landmarks of the area. The tree-lined plaza is set in a star-shaped landscape that represents the states and federal territories of the nation. The Perdana Putra (the office of the prime minister) is a six-story complex overlooking Putrajaya Lake. Topped with a graceful blue

A view of Malaysia's administrative capital, Putrajaya. Construction of the city is not expected to be completed until 2010.

dome, the building features a blend of European, Malay, and Islamic architecture. Also located in Putrajaya is Seri Perdana Complex, which holds the official residence of Malaysia's prime minister and the spectacular Putra Mosque. Constructed of rose-tinted granite, the mosque is a stunning representation of Persian architecture and can accommodate up to 15,000 people. The five tiers of the mosque represent both the five pillars of Islam and the five calls to prayer, which ring out over the city each day.

Cyberjaya is a smart city located near Putrajaya. "Where man and technology live in harmony" is the city's motto, and when Cyberjaya was

Mahathir bin Mohamad speaks at the official opening of Cyberjaya in 1999. This high-technology city is the nucleus of the Multimedia Super Corridor, which is located south of Kuala Lumpur.

officially opened in 1999, the landmark event was witnessed by 25 of the world's foremost leaders in the IT industry. The Multimedia University, known locally as MMU, was introduced as a flagship component of the city. Currently there are two MMU campuses—one in Cyberjaya, the other in Melaka. Through computer and web-based interactive learning programs, the MMU produces graduates who enter the fields of multimedia and advanced technology.

The city is a work-in-progress as it works toward developing into a fully equipped, self-sustaining cosmopolitan city. The City Command Centre (CCC) will be the electronic "brain" of the city, and is being designed to monitor and manage the public services (such as transportation, communications, and utilities) in a seamless system. As Malaysia's hub of international IT companies, Cyberjaya welcomes new residents from all over the world. In 2008, there were 37,000 reported residents in the city; Malaysian experts predict that by 2011 the city will support a residential population of over 120,000 people.

Melaka

While Kuala Lumpur and the MSC symbolize Malaysia's hope for the future, Melaka represents the nation's historic past. This quiet seaside city is located along the Malacca Strait, about 150 miles (241 km) south of Kuala Lumpur, and was home to more than 730,000 residents in 2009.

Melaka changed hands many times as European powers vied for control of the city, and Portuguese, Dutch, and British influences can be seen in the city's colonial architecture. Built by the Portuguese, A Fomasa was the first European settlement in Melaka. Although the fort was damaged during the Dutch invasion, it still stands today. The Portuguese influence is especially evident in Melaka's houses. Because the Portuguese taxed buildings according to their width, many people built homes and businesses that were narrow yet deep. A house that is only 12 feet (4 meters) wide can extend back for over 100 feet (30 meters), and may include several interior courtyards.

One of the most famous historic buildings in Melaka is the Stadthyus, built by the Dutch in 1650 as the official residence of the colonial authorities. The well-preserved building now houses the Historic Museum and Ethnography Museum and features a dazzling collection of relics from Melaka's multicultural past. The city is also home to some of the oldest functioning houses of worship in the country. The Cheng Hoon Teng Temple, the oldest Chinese temple in Malaysia, was founded in 1646 by Lee Wei King and built with materials shipped from southern China. The Masjid Kampung Hulu is the oldest functioning mosque in Malaysia still

The Kampung Keling Mosque in Melaka incorporates elements of Malay and Chinese architecture, such as the pagoda-style minaret to the left.

in its original location. The Dutch commissioned the mosque in 1728 to demonstrate its new policy of religious tolerance. The bright red Christ Church, built by the Dutch in 1753, is Malaysia's oldest Christian church.

Although the Europeans left their mark on Melaka, it is the Chinese influence that is most visible today. Bukit China (Chinese Hill), located on the outskirts of the city, is the largest Chinese graveyard outside of China. It was originally the site of the first permanent Chinese settlers in Malaysia. The descendants of these settlers are known today as the Baba Nyonya. Their history and culture is preserved in the Baba Nyonya Heritage Museum.

Johor Baharu

Johor Baharu is the capital of Johor, an important agricultural state producing valuable commodities such as rubber, palm oil, and pineapple. The state has also developed its industrial base, and as a result the population of its major cities has increased. With a population of approximately 900,000 people in 2009, Johor Baharu is currently the second-largest city in Malaysia. It is also the southernmost city in Peninsular Malaysia. A causeway and a railway link the city to Singapore, which lies across the Johor Strait.

Abu Bakar is known as the father of modern Johor. Shortly after the British formally acknowledged him as the sultan of Johor in 1855, he moved the state capital to Tanjung Puteri and renamed it Johor Baharu (meaning "New Johor"). One of the first major buildings the sultan commissioned was the Istana Besar ("Grand Palace"), built in 1866. Formerly the residence of the royal family, the palace now houses the Abu Bakar Royal Museum. Founded by Johor's present leader, Sultan Iskandar al-Haj, the museum features an extensive collection of royal treasures, including a display of cultural artifacts collected by the royal family during its reign. The Sultan Abu Bakar Mosque was completed in 1900 after eight years of construction and is hailed as one of the most beautiful mosques in Malaysia. Sultan Abu Bakar laid the first stone for the mosque, but passed away a few years before it was completed. The sultan's visions and

> The Handicraft Village and Craft Museum is located in Kota Baharu, the capital city of Kelantan. The museum's visitors can watch demonstrations of traditional handicrafts such as embroidery, songket weaving, batik, metalsmithing, and wood carving.

accomplishments are commemorated in the Sultan Abu Bakar Monument. A bronze replica of the Johor royal crown adorns this majestic building, located along the waterfront.

Other Major Cities

Shah Alam (population approximately 585,000) replaced Kuala Lumpur as the capital of Selangor after Kuala Lumpur was made a federal territory. Located about 19 miles (30 km) west of the nation's capital, Shah Alam has been the center of the palm oil industry for centuries and is also home to the Proton car company's main manufacturing plant. The city boasts the world's only agroforestry park, called the Bukit Cahaya Seri Aman Agricultural Park. This park lets visitors see how agroforestry works amid a natural wonderland of trees, birds, and animals. The park also features a biodome where visitors can experience all four seasons from summer to winter. The Sultan Salahuddin Abdul Aziz Shah Mosque, located in the city center, can be seen from miles away and features the tallest minarets in the world. Often called the "Blue Mosque," the central dome is one of the largest of its kind in the world.

Kuching is the capital of Sarawak, the largest state in Malaysia. Located on the banks of the Sarawak River, the city is home to an estimated 634,500 people. The Sarawak River has been the central hub of transportation, communication, and trade since ancient times and still plays an important role in the city's economy. The Kuching Waterfront, a beautifully landscaped boardwalk along the riverbank, is the main gathering place for city residents. During the mid-1980s, the Sarawak government focused on industrializing the economy of Kuching and other major cities in the state. Today a number of industries thrive in the city, including timber and food processing, metalwork, machinery assembly, and shipbuilding.

Kota Kinabalu (population approximately 579,300), formerly called Jesselton, is the capital of Sabah. The city was almost completely

The name of Sarawak's capital city, Kuching, literally means "cat" in Malay, and the city boasts the only museum in the world dedicated solely to cats.

destroyed during World War II but has emerged as the gateway to East Malaysia.

Labuan, another of Malaysia's federal territories, is an island located off the coast of Sabah. In 1990, it was declared an International Offshore Financial Center for the country, offering international investors some of the lowest corporate tax rates in the world. Labuan is populated by about 85,000 people. Today the island is fast becoming a popular tourist resort.

Ipoh (population approximately 711,000) is the capital of Perak, once the richest tin-mining region in the world. While not as developed as much as Malaysia's other large cities, Ipoh boasts some of the oldest cave temples in the country. Located north of Ipoh is the historical city of Taiping, famous for many firsts. Its Perak Museum was the first museum in Malaysia; the country's first railway ran from Taiping to Port Weld; and Bukit Larut (Maxwell Hill) is Malaysia's oldest hill resort.

Known as the "Pearl of the Orient," Penang Island is located off the northeastern coast of Peninsular Malaysia. Georgetown, the capital of Penang Island, was the first British settlement in Malaysia and prospered as a major trading port. Today the city is home to about 678,000 people and is famous for its elegant British colonial buildings as well as its pristine beaches.

Malaysia's former prime minister, Abdullah Ahmad Badawi (bottom left), escorts the heads of delegations from other Muslim countries to a meeting of the Organization of the Islamic Conference (OIC) in Putrajaya. As a leading member of the OIC, Malaysia holds an important position in the Muslim world.

7

Foreign Relations

*M*alaysia's leaders have always felt that a stable political, social, and economic environment is crucial to the forward progress of any nation. While domestic policies have focused on improving the lives of Malaysians, the government has tried to work with other developing countries on projects that are mutually beneficial, believing that economically successful neighbors are preferable to poor ones. Under the leadership of Mahathir bin Mohamad, Malaysia implemented a policy he called "prosper-thy-neighbor," by seeking mutually beneficial *bilateral* agreements with neighboring countries. "If you help your neighbor to prosper, you will prosper along with it," Mahathir told representatives of the World Bank in

Hong Kong at a 1997 meeting. "When countries are prosperous, they become more stable and their people need not emigrate to your country. Instead, their prosperity provides you with a market for your goods, with opportunities to invest and to enrich yourself even as you create jobs and wealth for them." Prime Minister Ahmad Badawi is expected to continue this policy.

Malaysia was a founding member of the Association of the Southeast Asian Nations (AESAN), along with Indonesia, the Philippines, Singapore, and Thailand. The purpose of the organization, which was formed in 1967, was to promote economic development, ensure political security and stability in the region, and foster cooperation among member countries. It also serves as a forum for the resolution of regional disagreements. During the 1990s, Malaysia helped to bring Laos, Vietnam, Cambodia, and Myanmar (formerly Burma) into the organization; it currently includes 10 states of Southeast Asia. In October 2003, leaders of the ASEAN nations signed a declaration called the Second Bali Concord, in which they agreed to pursue closer economic integration by 2020. Part of this proposal called for the establishment of a regional free-trade area. Today, the ASEAN region has a population of more than 560 million, a total area of 4.5 million square kilometers, a combined gross domestic product of almost US$1.1 trillion, and a total trade of about US$1.4 trillion.

Malaysia's leaders have often stressed that regional cooperation through organizations like ASEAN is an essential part of a larger global picture. For example, the ASEAN nations put into force the UN-backed International Ship and Port Facility Security Code in July 2004. This security measure, intended to protect shipping from terrorists, is sure to affect the future national security policies of Malaysia and its neighbors. Asia is home to some of the world's busiest ports, located in Hong Kong, Singapore, China, and Taiwan. The UN views this region as an excellent location to test the effectiveness of the new policy. Early reports revealed that a majority of ports were compliant with the policy.

The Malacca Strait, the key sea-lane between the Indian and Pacific Oceans, is bordered by Singapore, Indonesia, and Malaysia. About one-third of the world's sea traffic passes through the narrow channel, carrying about half of the world's oil supply. A lapse in security in any one of the nations bordering the narrow channel could result in a far-reaching destabilization of the industrialized world. Singapore, in particular, has consistently warned that terrorists may be planning to hijack ships for an incursion that could resemble the September 2001 attacks on the United States.

Malaysian marine police stop a small boat for inspection in the Malacca Strait. This narrow waterway is one of the busiest shipping lanes in the world. In recent years the governments of Malaysia and other countries that border the strait have worked to improve security in the strait.

In 2004, Malaysia took measures to boost security in the Malacca Strait by accepting an offer from the U.S. Navy to share intelligence and maintain joint counterterrorism exercises. However, both the United States and Malaysia made it very clear that there would be no U.S. or joint military patrols of the waters. The U.S. military's suggestions in April 2004 that it was considering sending troops to patrol the strait were met with anger and mistrust by Indonesian and Malaysian leaders. They warned that such action would only heighten anti-U.S. sentiment in the region and ultimately increase the terrorist threat. The United States maintains friendly relations with Indonesia and Malaysia and in June 2004 Admiral Thomas Fargo, U.S. military commander of the Pacific, assured Najib Razak, then Malaysia's minister of defense, that the United States "respects the sovereignty and territorial integrity of Malaysia." Although Malaysia has declared full support for the U.S.-led war against terrorism, it is still highly critical of U.S. methods.

Relations with the Islamic World

Malaysia's foreign relations with the Muslim world really took root after 1971, when Tunku Abdul Rahman became the first secretary-general of the Organization of the Islamic Conference (OIC). The Organization of the Islamic Conference, formed in 1969, is made up of more than 50 states with mostly Muslim populations. According to the organization's website, its goals are to strengthen Islamic solidarity among member states by promoting cooperation in the political, economic, social, cultural, and scientific fields; to support the struggle of the Palestinian people; and to eliminate discrimination and all forms of colonialism.

Tunku cultivated friendships with powerful and wealthy Arab nations, and initiated a variety of programs to promote Muslim unity both at home and abroad. His domestic projects included building Islamic schools and mosques, most of which were funded by wealthy Arab states. Other Malaysian leaders have continued this trend, and under the leadership of former prime minister Mahathir, the country formed ties with a number of Islamic countries. Mahathir maintained that a united and effective OIC was vital in a global economy dominated by non-Islamic powers.

During the 1990s, Mahathir established a number of economic partnerships, trade agreements, and investment contracts between Malaysia and OIC members such as Saudi Arabia and the United Arab Emirates (UAE). As a result, Malaysia's economic ties with the Islamic world have grown significantly. The country's volume of trade with other Islamic nations still remains relatively small, but it has shown substantial growth in the past five years. Malaysia's trade relations with Lebanon increased by over 30 percent between 2000 and 2001, and trade with Turkey totaled 1 billion ringgits in 2002. During the late 1990s, Malaysia also began investing directly in Islamic countries. Petronas, Malaysia's state-owned gas and oil company, has entered into a variety of partnerships with major oil-producing states like Algeria and Sudan. In Sudan, Petronas was involved with the Muglad Basin oil development project, which was completed in 1999. Since 1998, Malaysia has emerged as Sudan's second-largest foreign investor after China.

The Islamic Development Bank (IDB) has become more visible in recent years in a variety of developing nations, including Malaysia. Established in 1973 by the finance ministers of the OIC, the IDB's main objective is to promote socioeconomic development in Islamic countries. Funding for most of the IDB's projects comes from member states of the OIC. In 1990 the IDB launched a program called the Fund to assist and advance its investment activities. The IDB manages the Fund in accordance with *mudarabah*, the Islamic concept of partnership investment. Under a *mudarabah* partnership, one party provides investment capital and another party provides expertise and management. Profits are shared on a pre-established basis but losses are borne only by the investor.

Since its creation, the Fund has invested in a number of large-scale projects designed to spur the economic development of Islamic nations, including the construction of steel processing plants in Egypt and power plants in Pakistan and Turkey. Empowering the global Muslim community through research and knowledge remains a high priority of the IDB. The organization has financed the construction of a number of educational institutions including the University of Malaysia Sabah (UMS). In 2002, the IDB approved over a hundred projects totaling $512 million for Malaysia. Projects included equipping and upgrading hospitals and fire departments, as well as financing cutting-edge research equipment and teaching facilities for the University of Technology Malaysia (UTM) in Johor.

Malaysia has also reached out politically to help Muslims in other countries. In recent years, the Malaysian government participated in peace talks between the Moro Islamic Liberation Front, a Muslim anti-government insurgency in the Philippines, and the Philippine government.

Today, Malaysia views many Islamic nations, particularly those of the Arab world, as having vast potential to succeed in the global economy. However, Malaysian leaders have often pointed out that most Islamic countries place too much emphasis on religious education and not enough emphasis on career-oriented subjects such as science, mathematics, and—most importantly—technology. Malaysia's leaders warn that if Muslim nations remain economically backward, the dominant Western powers will continue to ignore their views on vital global issues.

Terrorism in Southeast Asia

Because Malaysia is a Muslim country, the beliefs of Islam play a large role in governmental and social issues. In the present era, Malaysia faces the challenges of growing Islamic fundamentalism and terrorism. Most Malaysians are moderate Muslims and want nothing to do with the militant Islamic sects that are terrorizing the region and other parts of the world. There is a strong sense of national unity, and most Malaysian Muslims feel that they are Malaysian first, Muslim second. However, there have been isolated militant groups that have drawn from the small numbers of fundamentalists in Malaysia. Islamic terrorist cells, such as the al-Qaeda group Jemaah Islamiyah (JI), have sprung up all over Southeast Asia, and the region has become a focal point in the U.S.-led war against terror. United under the banner of jihad ("holy war"), the terrorists believe that armed struggle is the only way to bring "pure Islam" back into the world, and that it is the duty of every Muslim to wage such a war.

Malaysia's neighbor, Indonesia, is the largest Muslim nation in the world. In recent years that country has suffered a string of bloody attacks, such as a 2002 bombing in Bali that killed 202 people (mostly foreign tourists), and the 2003 suicide bombing of a Marriott Hotel in Jakarta that claimed 13 lives. Authorities link these events to Jemaah Islamiyah (JI). According to Singapore's Ministry of Home Affairs, JI is also suspected of plotting to blow up the U.S. embassy in Singapore along with other targeted sites in the nation. It is believed that the group sought to blame Malaysia for these acts of aggression. The immediate goal of JI was to cause severe friction between Singapore and Malaysia, as well as between Malaysia and United States; its ultimate goal was the overthrow of the Malaysian government and the formation of an Islamic state encompassing Malaysia, Indonesia, and the Philippines. These plans were thwarted; however, JI is still suspected of having ties with the Malaysian terrorist cell Kumpulan Mujahidin Malaysia (KMM). Established in 1995 by an Afghani named Zainon Ismail, the KMM is also believed to have coordinated efforts with the extremely radical group Mujahedden Kompak in Indonesia. The KMM has allegedly sent members to help the Mujahedden Kompak in terrorizing the Christian population. In June 2007 authorities in Jakarta, Indonesia arrested JI's military commander, Abu Dujana, and seven other group members. He was later found guilty of conspiracy to commit terrorist attacks, harboring fugitives and stockpiling illegal arms.

World Relations

According to Malaysia's Ministry of Foreign Affairs, certain basic principles provide guidance in Malaysia's relations with the global community: "sovereign equality and mutual respect for territorial integrity, mutual non-aggression, non-interference in each other's internal affairs, peaceful settlement of disputes as well as mutual benefit in relations and peaceful co-existence." Malaysian leaders remained loyal to the principle of peaceful settlement in 1997 when they agreed to let the World Court settle a decades-old land dispute with Indonesia over Sipadan and Ligitan, two islands off the coast off Borneo. The court ruled in Malaysia's favor during 2002.

Malaysia maintains a number of international affiliations, including the membership in the United Nations (UN), the World Bank, the International Monetary Fund (IMF), the International Atomic Energy Agency, and the British Commonwealth of Nations. Malaysia is also a member of the Asia-Pacific Economic Cooperation (APEC). The country's leaders view their membership in these organizations as useful forums to air their views on vital global issues such as human rights, the environment, terrorism, nuclear disarmament, and the reform of the UN Security Council.

In 1999–2000, Malaysia served a two-year stint as a non-permanent member of the UN Security Council, the organization's most powerful body. During this time, Mahathir repeatedly protested the UN-imposed trade sanctions against Iraq and urged the Security Council to formulate a new program for monitoring Iraq's weapons program. According to Mahathir, the U.S.-led trade sanctions, which were imposed after Iraq invaded Kuwait in 1990, and the subsequent U.S. military actions against Iraq were exaggerated and unnecessary.

During the 2003 meeting of the UN General Assembly, Mahathir and other leaders from the developing world pressed for reform of the Security Council. Mahathir declared, "[The General Assembly] is unfortunately subservient to the Security Council, which in turn is subservient to any single one of the five victors of war fought more than half a century ago." The "five victors"—the United States, Russia, Britain, France, and China—are the only permanent members of the Security Council and have sole veto powers. Mahathir and other world leaders expressed their belief that developing countries should be granted authority to play a greater role in settling disputes among states.

As a leading member of the Non-Aligned Movement (NAM), Malaysia maintains a firm stance of non-interference and non-aggression with regard to other nations' internal affairs. As a result, the government maintains economic relations with countries even when it may not agree with their policies and actions. For example, Malaysia has long been an outspoken critic of U.S. foreign policies, particularly

Delegates attend a meeting of the Non-Aligned Movement (NAM) in Putrajaya. The Non-Aligned Movement was developed during the Cold War, and includes countries like Malaysia that refused to align with either the United States or Soviet Union.

regarding U.S. support of Israel and the 2003 invasion of Iraq. However, Malaysia maintains strong economic ties with the United States, and Mahathir visited the White House in 2002, where President George W. Bush thanked him for supporting the "war on terror."

The United States remains Malaysia's largest trading partner as well as its largest foreign investor. Malaysia also continues to play an active role in the World Trade Organization (WTO) and plans to continue developing economic relations with other nations in Asia, Africa, Latin America, and the Middle East. Although Malaysia is seeking new trade channels, it does not plan to neglect its traditional trading partners, which include the

Badawi meets U.S. President George W. Bush at the White House, July 2004. Although the United States and Malaysia have strong ties when it comes to trade, the two countries often differ over political issues. Malaysia's government was very critical of the U.S. invasion and subsequent occupation of Iraq, for example.

United States, Singapore, Japan, the European Union (EU), China, and Thailand. Currently, Israel is the only country with which Malaysia refuses to trade. According to the Ministry of Foreign Affairs, "Malaysia would consider beginning relations with Israel when a comprehensive peace agreement between Israel and the PLO is successfully concluded."

In the present era, terrorism and the proliferation of weapons of mass destruction (WMDs) are major areas of concern in virtually every corner of the globe. A vital component of Malaysia's foreign policy is geared toward promoting the signing and ratification of international agreements such as the Nuclear Non-Proliferation Treaty (NPT), Comprehensive Test Ban Treaty (CTBT), Biological Weapons Convention (BWC), Chemical Weapons Convention (CWC), and the Convention on Land Mines (CLM). On the home front, Malaysia is doing its part in the global war against terror. Dozens of suspected terrorists have been arrested and detained, and Malaysia has also beefed up border security in the northern hinterlands adjoining Thailand.

Globalization will continue to impact and mold Malaysia's foreign policy. As a developing country, Malaysia has both the opportunity and the responsibility to set an example as a forward-thinking, prosperous, and peaceful Islamic nation. Malaysia's most essential objectives regarding foreign relations were listed in a 1999 public statement by the Ministry of Foreign Affairs: "to contribute towards making the world much more peaceful and equitable, to provide leadership within our region and to demonstrate exemplary and responsible membership of the international community."

ca. 98,000 B.C.	The earliest human inhabitants of Peninsular Malaysia settle in the Lenggong Valley of Perak.
ca. 38,000 B.C.	Ancestors of the present-day Dayak peoples arrive in Sarawak and settle in the Mulu Caves.
ca. 3000 B.C.	According to archaeological evidence, inhabitants of the Lenggong Valley were working bronze and iron at this time, making them among the first Southeast Asians to use metal.
ca. 300 B.C.	Ancestors of present-day Malay people arrive from India, China, the Middle East, Indonesia, Thailand, and other neighboring regions by sea and overland routes.
200 B.C.	Early Malay kingdoms begin to emerge in Peninsular Malaysia.
A.D. 100	Traders from India and China arrive in Peninsular Malaysia.
200–1400	Buddhist-Malay and Hindu-Malay kingdoms flourish in Peninsular Malaysia; various states undergo "Indianization" as Buddhism and Hinduism spread throughout the region.
1400	Srivijayan prince Parameswara founds port city of Melaka.
1403	The first official trade envoy from China's Ming emperor arrives in Melaka.
1409	Admiral Zheng He, commander of the Chinese imperial fleet, leads second official trade envoy to Melaka.
1414	Parameswara marries a Muslim princess from Indonesia, embraces Islam, and changes his name to Raja Iskandar Shah; after his conversion Islam spreads rapidly throughout Malaysia.

Chronology

1511	After a Portuguese fleet conquers Melaka, the region becomes a Portuguese colony.
1641	The Dutch and their allies from Johor capture Melaka, making it a Dutch colony.
1786	British East India Company acquires Penang Island from the sultan of Kedah.
1826	Britain consolidates Penang Island, Singapore, and Melaka to form the Straits Settlements.
1841	Englishman James Brooke becomes raja of Sarawak.
1867	The Straits Settlements becomes a crown colony; British begin widespread development of British Malaya.
1896	British consolidate colonial holdings into the Federated Malay States.
1941–45	Japanese forces occupy the Malay states.
1946	Britain resumes control of the Malaya colony; Sarawak and Sabah formally cede their sovereignty to the British.
1948	The Malayan Communist Party (MCP) begins 12-year insurgency against British colonial government.
1955	First general elections are held in Peninsular Malaysia; the Alliance Party claims landslide victory.
1957	Malaysia gains independence from Britain on August 31; Tunku Abdul Rahman becomes the federation's first prime minister.
1963	Singapore, Sarawak, and Sabah join the independent federation of Malaya; the new federation (composed of 14 states) is renamed Malaysia on September 16; a two-year period of tensions with Indonesia, known as the Confrontation, begins.

1965	Singapore peacefully withdraws from Malaysia.
1967	Malaysia, Singapore, Indonesia, the Philippines, and Thailand form the Association of Southeast Asian Nations (ASEAN).
1969	Race riots erupt in Kuala Lumpur following general elections; Malaysian government declares a state of national emergency.
1970	Parliament reconvenes and Tun Abdul Razak becomes Malaysia's second prime minister; former prime minster Tunku Abdul Rahman becomes the first secretary-general of the Organization of the Islamic Conference (OIC).
1972	The Malaysian government launches the New Economic Policy (NEP), which is intended to redistribute some of the country's wealth to its majority Malay population.
1976	Hussein Onn becomes Malaysia's prime minister.
1981	Onn retires, and is replaced as prime minister Mahathir bin Mohamad.
1983	The East-West Highway opens in Peninsular Malaysia.
1985	The first Proton Saga, Malaysia's national car, rolls off the assembly line.
1993	Parti Islam Semalaysia (PAS) attempts to impose Islamic law (*Sharia*) after winning legislative control over the state of Kelantan, but the federal government blocks the effort.
1996	Malaysia celebrates the opening of Menara Kuala Lumpur, Asia's tallest telecommunications tower; the country launches its first satellite and direct-to-home satellite TV.

Chronology

1999	The Petronas Twin Towers in Kuala Lumpur officially open, as does Cyberjaya in the Multimedia Super Corridor (MSC); Putrajaya becomes new administrative capital of Malaysia.
1999–2000	Malaysia serves as a non-permanent member of the U.N. Security Council.
2002	President George W. Bush praises Malaysia for its support in the U.S.-led war against terrorism.
2003	In a widely publicized speech, Mahathir accuses the United States of using its war against terror to "dominate the world" and demands that the U.S. not attack Iraq; Mahathir steps down as prime minister in October, and Abdullah bin Ahmad Badawi becomes Malaysia's fifth prime minister.
2004	Malaysia agrees to work with the U.S. Navy to boost security in the Malacca Strait.
2005	Malaysia's government contributes to relief efforts to help the survivors of the tsunami that devastated communities throughout Southeast Asia, particularly Indonesia.
2006	In December, Sultan Mizan Zainal Abidin installed as Malaysia's 13th king in December.
2007	Malaysia is rocked by two anti-government rallies: the 2007 Bersih Rally for electoral reform; and the 2007 HINDRAF Hindu Rights Action Force Rally, which protested alleged discriminatory policies which favored ethnic Malays.
2008	Badawi's governing coalition loses its two-thirds majority in March 2008 parliamentary elections.
2009	Najib Tun Razak is sworn in as Malaysia's prime minister on April 3.

animism—the belief in the existence of spirits within nature and inanimate objects.

Austronesian—native inhabitants of the Austronesian islands of the South Pacific, including Indonesia, Melanesia, Micronesia, and Polynesia.

bilateral—two-sided; mutual.

biodiversity hotspot—an area that features exceptional concentrations of diverse species, including many endemic or native species found only in those regions.

communist—an advocate of a government system based on collective ownership.

confluence—the flowing together of two or more streams.

globalization—the mass increase in connections between countries for the sake of cultural and economic exchange.

gross domestic product (GDP)—the total value of goods and services that a country produces in one year.

meritocracy—a system of government and society based upon individual ability or achievement rather than by race, wealth, or social position.

oxbow lake—a distinctively curved lake formed when a meandering stream or river is cut off.

parasitic—relating to an organism that lives in, with, or on another organism.

protectorate—a country or region that shares authority with a superior power in exchange for protection from invasion.

raja—a prince, chief, or ruler in India or the East Indies.

subsistence—the minimum necessary to support life.

sultanate—a state or country governed by a sultan.

typhoon—a tropical cyclone occurring in the western sections of the Pacific Ocean.

Further Reading

Frankham, Steve. *Malaysia and Singapore: Tread Your Own Path*. Bath, UK: Footprint Handbooks, 2008.

Gatsiounis, Ioannis. *Beyond the Veneer: Malaysia's Struggle for Dignity and Direction*. Singapore: Monsoon Books, 2008.

Hooker, Virginia Matheson. *Malaysia: Islam, Society, and Politics*. Pasir Panjang, Singapore: Institute of Southeast Asian Studies, 2003.

Hutton, Wendy, and Luca Invernizzi Tettoni. *Authentic Recipes from Malaysia*. Singapore: Peripus Editions, 2005.

Manicka, Rani. *The Rice Mother*. New York: Penguin Books, 2004.

Moore, Wendy. *Malaysia: A Pictorial History, 1400–2004*. Singapore: Didier Millet, 2007.

Munan, Heidi. *Culture Shock! Malaysia: A Survival Guide to Customs and Etiquette*. New York: Marshall Cavendish, 2008.

http://www.parlimen.gov.my/eng-pengenalan-lblakng.htm

The official Web site of Malaysia's parliament includes an introduction, news, and links to other pages related to both houses of the assembly.

http://www3.pmo.gov.my

This page managed by the office of the prime minister includes news, announcements, and speeches by government leaders.

http://www.kln.gov.my/

The Malaysian Ministry of Foreign Affairs includes information about Malaysia's domestic and foreign policies.

http://www.statistics.gov.my/

The Malaysia Department of Statistics offers statistics on population, employment, trade, and other matters.

http://www.lonelyplanet.com/destinations/south_east_asia/ malaysia/

This Lonely Planet Web page provides historical and cultural information on Malaysia's best-known locations.

http://www.interknowledge.com/malaysia/

This page has excellent information on a broad range of topics, including Malaysia's history, natural habitats, and annual events.

Index

Numbers in **bold italic** refer to captions.

Index

Picture Credits

The **FOREIGN POLICY RESEARCH INSTITUTE (FPRI)** served as editorial consultants for the MAJOR MUSLIM NATIONS series. FPRI is one of the nation's oldest "think tanks." The Institute's Middle East Program focuses on Gulf security, monitors the Arab-Israeli peace process, and sponsors an annual conference for teachers on the Middle East, plus periodic briefings on key developments in the region.

Among the FPRI's trustees is a former Secretary of State and a former Secretary of the Navy (and among the FPRI's former trustees and interns, two current Undersecretaries of Defense), not to mention two university presidents emeritus, a foundation president, and several active or retired corporate CEOs.

The scholars of FPRI include a former aide to three U.S. Secretaries of State, a Pulitzer Prize–winning historian, a former president of Swarthmore College and a Bancroft Prize–winning historian, and two former staff members of the National Security Council. And the FPRI counts among its extended network of scholars—especially its Inter-University Study Groups—representatives of diverse disciplines, including political science, history, economics, law, management, religion, sociology, and psychology.

DR. HARVEY SICHERMAN is president and director of the Foreign Policy Research Institute in Philadelphia, Pennsylvania. He has extensive experience in writing, research, and analysis of U.S. foreign and national security policy, both in government and out. He served as Special Assistant to Secretary of State Alexander M. Haig Jr. and as a member of the Policy Planning Staff of Secretary of State James A. Baker III. Dr. Sicherman was also a consultant to Secretary of the Navy John F. Lehman Jr. (1982–1987) and Secretary of State George Shultz (1988).

A graduate of the University of Scranton (B.S., History, 1966), Dr. Sicherman earned his Ph.D. at the University of Pennsylvania (Political Science, 1971), where he received a Salvatori Fellowship. He is author or editor of numerous books and articles, including *America the Vulnerable: Our Military Problems and How to Fix Them* (FPRI, 2002) and *Palestinian Autonomy, Self-Government and Peace* (Westview Press, 1993). He edits *Peacefacts*, an FPRI bulletin that monitors the Arab-Israeli peace process.

BARBARA AOKI POISSON is the author of *The Ainu of Japan* (Lerner, 2002) and *Ghana* (Mason Crest, 2004). She is a freelance journalist who has published hundreds of articles in newspapers and magazines such as *The Mariner*, *The Antiquer*, and *Family Fun*. She lives in Leonardtown, Maryland.